Poet to Poet
Whitman Selected by Robert Creeley

Walt Whitman (1819–92) started his literary life as a New York
journalist. By the age of thirty-five he had become America's
national poet and an almost mythical figure as the hero of his
astonishing *Leaves of Grass*, first published in 1855. *Leaves of
Grass* would have passed almost unnoticed had it not been
enthusiastically received by the Transcendentalists, especially
Emerson, who hailed it as 'the most extraordinary piece of wit
and wisdom that America has yet contributed'.

Robert Creeley was born in 1926 and is a poet, novelist,
short-story writer and one of America's most important poets
today. He is usually associated with the Black Mountain school
of American poetry and from 1954–7 he edited the *Black
Mountain Review*, which included those American writers who
have made the greatest mark in contemporary American
literature: William Carlos Williams, Charles Olson, Louis
Zukofsky, Allen Ginsberg, Jack Kerouac, Robert Duncan,
Ed Dorn, Gary Snyder and many others. His publications include
Words, *For Love*, and *Pieces*. Robert Creeley has also co-edited
with Donald Allen, *New American Story* and *The New Writing in
the U.S.A.* (both published by Penguins).

T: **WHITMAN**

Selected by

Robert Creeley

Penguin Books

Penguin Books Ltd, Harmondsworth,
Middlesex, England
Penguin Books Inc., 7110 Ambassador Road,
Baltimore, Maryland 21207, U.S.A.
Penguin Books Australia Ltd, Ringwood,
Victoria, Australia

This selection first published 1973
Copyright © Penguin Books Ltd, 1973
Introduction copyright © Robert Creeley, 1973

Made and printed in Great Britain by
Richard Clay (The Chaucer Press), Ltd,
Bungay, Suffolk
Set in Monotype Ehrhardt

Contents

Introduction

One of the most lovely insistences in Whitman's poems seems to me his instruction that one speak for oneself. Assumedly that would be the person most involved in saying anything and yet a habit of 'objective' statement argues the contrary, noting the biases and distortions and tediums of the personal that are thereby invited into the writing. Surely there is some measure possible, such would say, that can make statement a clearly defined and impersonal instance of reality, of white clouds in a blue sky, of things and feelings not distorted by any fact of one man or woman's intensive possession of them. Then there would truly be a common possibility, that all might share, and that no one would have use of more than another.

Yet if Whitman has taught me anything, and he has taught me a great deal, often against my own will, it is that the common *is* personal, intensely so, in that having no one thus to invest it, the sea becomes a curious mixture of water and table salt and the sky the chemical formula for air. It is, paradoxically, the personal which makes the common in so far as it recognizes the existence of the many in the one. In my own joy or despair, I am brought to that which others have also experienced.

My own senses of Whitman were curiously numb until I was thirty. In the forties, when I was in college, it was considered literally bad taste to have an active interest in his writing. In that sense he suffered the same fate as Wordsworth, also condemned as overly prolix and generalizing. There was a persistent embarrassment that this naively affirmative poet might affect one's own somewhat cynical wisdoms. Too, in so far as this was a time of intensively didactic criticism, what was one to do with Whitman, even if one read him? He went on and on, he seemed to lack 'structure', he yielded to no 'critical apparatus' then to hand. So, as students, we were herded past him as quickly as possible, and our teachers used him only as an example of 'the America of that period' which, we were told, was a vast swamp of idealistic expansion and corruption. Whitman, the dupe, the dumb-bell, the pathetically regrettable instance of this country's dream and despair, the self-taught man.

That summation of Whitman and his work was a very comfortable one for all concerned. If I felt at times awkward with it, I had only to turn to Ezra Pound, whom the university also condemned, to find that he too disapproved despite the begrudging 'Pact'. At least he spoke of having 'detested' Whitman, only publicly altering the implications of that opinion in a series of BBC interviews made in the late fifties. William Carlos Williams also seemed to dislike him, decrying the looseness of the writing, as he felt it, and the lack of a coherent prosody. He as well seemed to change his mind in age in so far as he referred to Whitman as the greatest of American poets in a public lecture on American poetry for college students. Eliot also changes his mind, as did James before him, but the point is that the heroes of my youth as well as my teachers were almost without exception extremely critical of Whitman and his influence and wanted as little as possible to do with him.

Two men, however, most dear to me, felt otherwise. The first of these was D. H. Lawrence, whose *Studies in Classic American Literature* remains the most extraordinary apprehension of the nature of American experience and writing that I know. His piece on Whitman in that book is fundamental in that he, in a decisively personal manner, first castigates Whitman for what he considers a muddling assumption of 'oneness', citing 'I am he that aches with amorous love . . .' as particularly offensive, and then, with equal intensity, applauds that Whitman who is, as he puts it, 'a great charger of the blood in men', a truly heroic poet whose vision and will make a place of absolute communion for others.

The second, Hart Crane, shared with Whitman my own teachers' disapproval. I remember a course which I took with F. O. Mathiessen, surely a man of deep commitment and care for his students, from which Crane had been absented. I asked for permission to give a paper on Crane, which he gave me, but I had overlooked what I should have realized would be the response of the class itself, understandably intent upon its own sophistications. How would they accept these lines, for example?

> yes, Walt,
> Afoot again, and onward without halt, –
> Not soon, nor suddenly, – no, never to let go
> My hand
> in yours,
> Walt Whitman –
> so –

If they did not laugh outright at what must have seemed to them the awkwardly stressed rhymes and sentimental camaraderie, then they tittered at Crane's will to be one with his fellow *homosexual*. But didn't they hear, I wanted to insist, the pacing of the rhythms of those lines, the syntax, the intently human tone, or simply the punctuation? Couldn't they read? Was Crane to be simply another 'crudity' they could so glibly be rid of? But still I myself didn't read Whitman, more than the few poems of his that were 'dealt with' in classes or that some friend asked me to. No doubt I too was embarrassed by my aunt's and my grandmother's ability to recite that terrible poem, 'O Captain! My Captain!', banal as I felt it to be, and yet what was that specious taste which could so distract any attention and could righteously dismiss so much possibility, just because it didn't 'like' it? Sadly, it was too much my own.

So I didn't really read Whitman for some years although from time to time I realized that the disposition toward his work must be changing. Increasing numbers of articles began to appear as, for one example, Randall Jarrell's 'Whitman Revisited'. But the import of this writing had primarily to do with Whitman's work as instance of social history or else with its philosophical basis or, in short, with all that did not attempt to respect the technical aspects of his writing, his prosody and the characteristic method of his organization within the specific poems.

It was, finally, the respect accorded Whitman by three of my fellow poets that began to impress me as not only significant to their various concepts of poetry but as unmistakable evidence of his basic use to any estimation of the nature of poetry itself. I had grown up, so to speak, habituated to the use of poetry as compact, epiphanal instance of emotion or insight. I valued its intensive compression, its ability to 'get through' a maze of conflict and confusion to some centre of clear 'point'. But what did one do if the emotion or terms of thought could not be so focused upon or isolated in such singularity? Assuming a context in which the statement was of necessity multiphasic, a circumstance the components of which were multiple, or, literally, a day in which various things *did* occur, not simply one thing – what did one do with that? Allen Ginsberg was quick to see that Whitman's line was of very specific use. As he says in 'Notes Written on Finally Recording Howl', 'No attempt's been made to use it in the light of early XX Century organization of new speech-rhythm prosody to *build up* large organic structures'. The structure of 'Howl' itself and of subsequent poems such as 'Kaddish' demonstrates to my own mind how much technically Ginsberg had learned from Whitman's method of taking the poem as a 'field', in Charles Olson's sense, rather than as a discreet line through alternatives to some adamant point of conclusion.

In the work of Robert Duncan the *imagination* of the poem is very coincident with Whitman's. For example, in a contribution to *Poets on Poetry* (1966) Duncan writes:

> We begin to imagine a cosmos in which the poet and the poem are one in a moving process, not only here the given Creation and the Exodus or Fall, but also here the immanence of the Creator in Creation. The most real is given and we have fallen away, but the most real is in the falling revealing itself in what is happening. Between the god *in* the story and the god *of* the story, the form, the realization of what is happening, stirs the poet. To answer that call, to become the poet, means to be aware of creation, creature and creator coinherent in the one event . . .

If one reads the 1855 'Preface' to *Leaves of Grass* in the context here defined, the seeming largenesses of act which Whitman grants to the poet find actual place in that 'immanence of the Creator in Creation' which Duncan notes. More, the singular presence of Whitman in Duncan's 'A Poem Beginning with a line by pindar' is an extraordinary realization of the *measure* Whitman has given us:

> . . . There is no continuity then. Only a few
>   posts of the good remain. I too
> that am a nation sustain the damage
>   where smokes of continual ravage
> obscure the flame.
>   It is across great scars of wrong
> I reach toward the song of kindred men
>   and strike again the naked string

old Whitman sang from. Glorious mistake!
  that cried:

'The theme is creative and has vista.'
'He is the president of regulation.'

I see always the under side turning,
fumes that injure the tender landscape.
  From which up break
lilac blossoms of courage in daily act
  striving to meet a natural measure.

Louis Zukofsky, the third friend thus to instruct me, recalls and transforms Whitman's *Leaves* again and again, as here:

The music is in the flower,
Leaf around leaf ranged around the center;
Profuse but clear outer leaf breaking on space,
There is space to step to the central heart:
The music is in the flower,
It is not the sea but hyaline cushions the flower –
Liveforever, everlasting.
The leaves never topple from each other,
Each leaf a buttress flung for the other.

(from '*A*' 2, 1928)

I have no way of knowing if those lines directly refer to Whitman's *Leaves of Grass* and yet, intuitively, I have no doubt of it whatsoever. Zukofsky once told me that, for him, the eleventh section of 'Song of Myself' constituted the American *Shih King*, which is to say, it taught the possibilities of what might be said or sung in poetry with that grace of technical agency, or mode, thereby to accomplish those possibilities. *It presents*. It does not talk about or refer to – in the subtlety of its realization, it becomes real.

It is also Zukofsky who made me aware of Whitman's power in an emotion I had not associated with him – a deeply passionate anger. Zukofsky includes an essay called 'Poetry' in the first edition of '*A*' *1–12* at the end of which he quotes the entire text of 'Respondez!', a poem which Whitman finally took out of *Leaves of Grass* in 1881 but which I have put in this selection, as singular instance of that power and in respect to the man who made me aware of it.

Then, in the late fifties, I found myself embarrassed for proper academic credentials although I was teaching at the time, and so went back to graduate school, to get the appropriate degree. One of the first courses I took in that situation was called 'Twain and Whitman', taught by John Gerber, who was a visiting professor at the University of New Mexico from Iowa State. One thing he did with us I remember very well – he asked us to do a so-called thematic outline of 'Song of Myself'. The room in which we met had large blackboards on all four walls and on the day they were due, we were told to copy our various outlines on to the blackboards. So we all got up and did so. When we finally got back to our seats, we noticed one very striking fact. No two of the outlines were the same – which was Professor Gerber's very instructive point. Whitman did not write with a systematized logic of 'subject' nor did he 'organize' his materials with a logically set schedule for their occurrence in the poem. Again the situation of a 'field' of activity, rather than some didactic imposition of a 'line' of order, was very clear.

At that same time I became interested in the nature of Whitman's prosody and looked through as many scholarly articles concerning it as I could find in the university library. None were really of much use to me, simply that the usual academic measure of such activity depends upon the rigid presumption of a standardized metrical system, which is, at best, the hindsight gained from a practice far more fluid in its own occasion. Sculley Bradley (co-editor with Harold W. Blodgett of the best text for Whitman's poems available to my knowledge: *Leaves of Grass*, Comprehensive Reader's Edition, New York University Press, 1965) did speak of a *variable stress* or *foot*, that is, a hovering accent, or accents, within clusters of words in the line that did not fall in a statically determined pattern but rather shifted with the impulse of the statement itself. This sense of the stress pattern in Whitman's poems was interestingly parallel to William Carlos Williams's use of what he also called 'the variable foot' in his later poems, so that the periodicity of the line, its duration in time, so to speak, stayed in the general pattern constant but the stress or stresses within the unit of the line itself were free to move with the condition of the literal things being said, both as units of semantic information, e.g., 'I am the chanter . . .', or as units of sound and rhythm, e.g., 'I chant copious the islands beyond . . .' It is, of course, impossible ever to separate these two terms in their actual function, but it is possible that one will be more or less concerned with each in turn in the activity of writing. More simply, I remember one occasion in high school when I turned a 'unit' primarily involved with sounds and rhythm into a 'unit' particularly involved with semantic statement, to wit: 'Inebriate of air am I . . .' altered in my memory to read, 'I am an inebriate of air . . .' My teacher told me I had the most unpoetic ear he'd yet encountered.

Remember that what we call 'rhyming' is the recurrence of a sound sufficiently similar to one preceding it to catch in the ear and mind as being the 'same' and that such sounds can be modified in a great diversity of ways. In the sounding of words themselves the extension seems almost endless: *maid*, *made*, *may*, *met*, *mad*, *mate*, *wait*, *say*, etc. Given the initial vowel with its accompanying consonants and also its own condition, i.e., whether it is 'long' or 'short', one can then play upon that sound as long as one's energy *and* the initial word's own ability to stay in the ear as 'residue' can survive. In verse the weaving and play of such sound is far more complex than any observation of the rhymes at the ends of lines can tabulate.

This kind of rhyming is instance of what one can call *parallelism*, and the parallelism which similarity of sounds can effect is only one of the many alternate sources of 'rhyming' which verse has at hand. For example, there is a great deal of syntactic 'rhyming' in Whitman's poetry, insistently parallel syntactic structures which themselves make a strong web of coherence. There is also the possibility of parallelism in the nature of what is being thought and/or felt as emotion, and this too can serve to increase the experience of coherence in the statement the poem is working to accomplish.

The constantly recurring structures in Whitman's writing, the insistently parallel sounds and rhythms, recall the patterns of waves as I now see them daily. How can I point to *this* wave, or *that* one, and announce that it is *the* one? Rather Whitman's method seems to me a process of sometimes seemingly endless gathering, moving in the energy of his own attention and impulse. There are obviously occasions to the contrary to be found in his work but the basic pattern does seem of this order. I am struck by the fact that William Michael Rossetti in the introduction to his *Poems of Walt Whitman* (1868) speaks of the style as being occasionally 'agglomerative', a word which can mean 'having the state of a confused or jumbled mass' but which, more literally, describes the circumstance of something 'made or formed into a rounded mass or ball'. A few days ago here, walking along the beach, a friend showed me such a ball, primarily of clay but equally compacted of shells and pebbles which the action of the waves had caused the clay to pick up, all of which would, in time, become stone. That meaning of 'agglomerate' I think particularly relevant to the activity of Whitman's composition, and I like too that sense of the spherical, which does not locate itself upon a point nor have the strict condition of the linear but rather is at all 'points' the possibility of all that it is. Whitman's constant habit of revisions and additions would concur, I think, with this notion of his process, in that there is not 'one thing' to be said and, that done, then 'another'. Rather the process permits the material ('myself' in the world) to extend until literal death intercedes. Again, it is interesting to think of Zukofsky's sense that any of us as poets 'write one poem all our lives', remembering that Whitman does not think of his work as a series of discreet collections or books but instead adds to the initial work, *Leaves of Grass*, thinking of it as a 'single poem'.

The implications of such a stance have a very contemporary bearing for American poets – who can no longer assume either their world or themselves in it as discrete occasion. Not only does Whitman anticipate the American affection for the pragmatic, but he equally emphasizes that it is space and process which are unremittingly our condition. If Pound found the manner of his poems objectionable, he nonetheless comes to a form curiously like *Leaves of Grass* in the *Cantos*, in that he uses them as the literal possibility of a life. Much the same situation occurs in Williams's writing with *Paterson*, although it comes at a markedly later time in his own writing. Charles Olson's *Maximus Poems* and Louis Zukofsky's '*A*' are also instances of this form which proposes to 'go on' in distinction to one that assumes its own containment as a singular case.

Another objection Rossetti had concerned what he called 'absurd or ill-constructed words' in Whitman's writing. One distinct power a poet may be blessed with is that of *naming* and Whitman's appetite in this respect was large and unembarrassed. One should read a posthumously published collection of notes he wrote on his own sense of words called *An American Primer* (City Lights, 1970), wherein he makes clear his commitment to their power of transformation. Whitman's vocabulary moves freely among an extraordinarily wide range of occupational terminologies and kinds of diction found in divers social groupings. Frequently there are juxta-positions of terms appropriate to markedly different social or occupational habits, slang sided with words of an alternate derivation:

> I chant the chant of dilation or pride,
> We have had ducking and deprecating about enough . . .

Whatever the reader's response, such language permits Whitman to gain an actively useful diversity of context and tone. The toughness of his verse – what Charles Olson referred to as its *muscularity*, giving as instance 'Trickle Drops' – can sustain the tensions created in its movement by these seeming disparities in diction. It is, moreover, a marked characteristic of American poetry since Whitman, and certainly of the contemporary, to have no single source for its language in the sense that it does not depend upon a 'poetic' or literary vocabulary. In contrast, a German friend once told me that even a novelist as committed to a commonly shared situation of life as Günter Grass could not be easily understood by the workmen whose circumstance so moved him. His language was too literary in its structures and vocabulary, not by fact of his own choice but because such language was adamantly that in which novels were to be written in German. An American may choose, as John Ashbery once did, to write a group of poems whose words come entirely from the diction of the *Wall Street Journal*, but it is his own necessity, not that put upon him by some rigidity of literary taste.

Comparable to this flexibility of diction in Whitman's writing is the tone or mood in which his poems speak. It is very open, familiar, at times very casual and yet able to be, on the instant, intensive, intimate, charged with complexly diverse emotion. This manner of address invites, as it were, the person reading to 'come into' the activity and experience of the poems, to share with Whitman in a paradoxically unsentimental manner the actual texture and force of the emotions involved. When he speaks directly to the reader, there is an uncanny feeling of his literal presence, physically.

I have avoided discussion of Whitman's life simply because I am not competent to add anything to the information of any simple biography, for example, Gay Wilson Allen's *Walt Whitman* (Evergreen Books, London, 1961). I am charmed by some of the details got from that book. Apparently Mrs Gilchrist, the widow of Blake's biographer, Alexander Gilchrist, was very smitten upon reading Whitman's poems and wrote accordingly:

Even in this first letter (3 September, 1871) Mrs Gilchrist made it plain that she was proposing marriage. She hoped, she said, to hear, 'My Mate. The one I so much want. Bride, Wife, indissoluble eternal!' And, 'Dear Walt. It is a sweet & precious thing, this love: it clings so close, so close to the Soul and Body, all so tenderly dear, so beautiful, so sacred . . .'

It is simple enough to make fun of this lady and yet her response, despite Whitman's very careful demurring, is one that his poems are unequivocally capable of producing. It would be sad indeed if books could not be so felt as entirely human and possible occasion.

More to the point, Whitman's life is a very discreet one, really. John Addington Symonds so pestered him concerning 'the meaning of the "Calamus" poems', that Whitman finally answered, 'Though unmarried, I have six children . . .' But whether or not that was true, or untrue, or whether Whitman was homosexual, bisexual, or heterosexual, has not primarily concerned me. In other words, I have been intent upon the writing and what there took place and that, literally, is what any of us have now as a possibility. We cannot haul him back any more than we can Shakespeare, just to tell us who he was. It would seem that he *had*, with such magnificent articulation one is almost persuaded there can be no end to him just as there is none to the genius of his writing.

Nor have I been able to do more than gloss the multiplicity of uses I find in the work itself. I wish there were time to think of Whitman as instance of what Allen Ginsberg pointed out as a great tradition of American poets, that of the *crank* or true eccentric. Surely his contemporaries often felt him to be. There is a lovely letter which Gerard Manley Hopkins wrote Bridges, in which he says that Whitman is closer to him in technical concerns than any other poet then writing – but also, that he is a veritable madman, so what does that make poor Hopkins? Or I would like to consider a suggestion of Duncan's, that possibly Williams's uneasiness with Whitman's writing had in part to do with the fact that Williams uses *enjambment*, or 'run-over' lines, very frequently whereas Whitman uses it not at all – wherein he is very like Ezra Pound. Or to trace more carefully the nature of Whitman's influence on American poetry – an influence I find as clearly in Frank O'Hara's poems as I do in Crane's or Ginsberg's.

Undertaking any of this, I felt a sudden giddiness – not at all self-humbling. This man is a *great* poet, our first, and it is unlikely indeed that his contribution to what it literally means to be an *American* poet will ever be equalled. But I do not want to end this note with such blatant emphasis. As Duncan says, Whitman is a deeply gentle man and, humanly, of great, great reassurance. If our America now is a petty shambles of disillusion and violence, the dreams of its possibility stay actual in Whitman's words. It is not 'democracy' that, of itself, can realize or even recognize the common need. It is only, and literally, people themselves who have that choice. So then, as Lawrence said: 'Ahead of all poets, pioneering into the wilderness of unopened life, Whitman . . .'

*

My selections were taken, with one exception, from Walt Whitman, *Leaves of Grass*, ed. Harold W. Blodgett and Sculley Bradley, New York University Press, 1965. 'The Sleepers' uses the text found in *Walt Whitman's Leaves of Grass, The First (1855) Edition*, ed. Malcolm Cowley, Secker & Warburg, London, 1960.

ROBERT CREELEY

Bolinas, California
30 January, 1972

Eidólons

    I met a seer,
Passing the hues and objects of the world,
The fields of art and learning, pleasure, sense,
    To glean eidólons.

    Put in thy chants said he,
No more the puzzling hour nor day, nor segments, parts,
    put in,
Put first before the rest as light for all and entrance-song
    of all,
    That of eidólons.

    Ever the dim beginning,
Ever the growth, the rounding of the circle,
Ever the summit and the merge at last, (to surely start
    again,)
    Eidólons! eidólons!

    Ever the mutable,
Ever materials, changing, crumbling, re-cohering,
Ever the ateliers, the factories divine,
    Issuing eidólons.

    Lo, I or you,
Or woman, man, or state, known or unknown,
We seeming solid wealth, strength, beauty build,
    But really build eidólons.

    The ostent evanescent,
The substance of an artist's mood or savan's studies long,
Or warrior's, martyr's, hero's toils,
    To fashion his eidólon.

Of every human life,
(The units gather'd, posted, not a thought, emotion, deed,
　　　left out,)
The whole or large or small summ'd, added up,
　　　In its eidólon.

The old, old urge,
Based on the ancient pinnacles, lo, newer, higher pinnacles,
From science and the modern still impell'd,
　　　The old, old urge, eidólons.

The present now and here,
America's busy, teeming, intricate whirl,
Of aggregate and segregate for only thence releasing,
　　　Today's eidólons.

These with the past,
Of vanish'd lands, of all the reigns of kings across the sea,
Old conquerors, old campaigns, old sailors' voyages,
　　　Joining eidólons.

Densities, growth, façades,
Strata of mountains, soils, rocks, giant trees,
Far-born, far-dying, living long, to leave,
　　　Eidólons everlasting.

Exaltè, rapt, ecstatic,
The visible but their womb of birth,
Of orbic tendencies to shape and shape and shape,
　　　The mighty earth-eidólon.

All space, all time,
(The stars, the terrible perturbations of the suns,
Swelling, collapsing, ending, serving their longer, shorter
　　　use,)
　　　Fill'd with eidólons only.

The noiseless myriads,
The infinite oceans where the rivers empty,
The separate countless free identities, like eyesight,
    The true realities, eidólons.

Not this the world,
Nor these the universes, they the universes,
Purport and end, ever the permanent life of life,
    Eidólons, eidólons.

Beyond thy lectures learn'd professor,
Beyond thy telescope or spectroscope observer keen, beyond
    all mathematics,
Beyond the doctor's surgery, anatomy, beyond the chemist
    with his chemistry,
    The entities of entities, eidólons.

Unfix'd yet fix'd,
Ever shall be, ever have been and are,
Sweeping the present to the infinite future,
    Eidólons, eidólons, eidólons.

The prophet and the bard,
Shall yet maintain themselves, in higher stages yet,
Shall mediate to the Modern, to Democracy, interpret yet
    to them,
    God and eidólons.

And thee my soul,
Joys, ceaseless exercises, exaltations,
Thy yearning amply fed at last, prepared to meet,
    Thy mates, eidólons.

Thy body permanent,
The body lurking there within thy body,
The only purport of the form thou art, the real I myself,
    An image, an eidólon.

Thy very songs not in thy songs,
No special strains to sing, none for itself,
But from the whole resulting, rising at last and floating,
    A round full-orb'd eidólon.

1876

To the States

To the States or any one of them, or any city of the States,
  Resist much, *obey little*,
Once unquestioning obedience, once fully enslaved,
Once fully enslaved, no nation, state, city of this earth,
  ever afterward resumes its liberty.

1860

Starting from Paumanok

I

Starting from fish-shape Paumanok where I was born,
Well-begotten, and rais'd by a perfect mother,
After roaming many lands, lover of populous pavements,
Dweller in Mannahatta my city, or on southern savannas,
Or a soldier camp'd or carrying my knapsack and gun, or
    a miner in California,
Or rude in my home in Dakota's woods, my diet meat, my
    drink from the spring,
Or withdrawn to muse and meditate in some deep recess,
Far from the clank of crowds intervals passing rapt and
    happy,
Aware of the fresh free giver the flowing Missouri, aware
    of mighty Niagara,
Aware of the buffalo herds grazing the plains, the hirsute
    and strong-breasted bull,
Of earth, rocks, Fifth-month flowers experienced, stars,
    rain, snow, my amaze,
Having studied the mocking-bird's tones and the flight of
    the mountain-hawk,
And heard at dawn the unrivall'd one, the hermit thrush
    from the swamp-cedars,
Solitary, singing in the West, I strike up for a New World.

2

Victory, union, faith, identity, time,
The indissoluble compacts, riches, mystery,
Eternal progress, the kosmos, and the modern reports.

This then is life,
Here is what has come to the surface after so many throes
    and convulsions.

How curious! how real!
Underfoot the divine soil, overhead the sun.

See revolving the globe,
The ancestor-continents away group'd together,
The present and future continents north and south, with
    the isthmus between.

See, vast trackless spaces,
As in a dream they change, they swiftly fill,
Countless masses debouch upon them,
They are now cover'd with the foremost people, arts,
    institutions, known.

See, projected through time,
For me an audience interminable.

With firm and regular step they wend, they never stop,
Successions of men, Americanos, a hundred millions,
One generation playing its part and passing on,
Another generation playing its part and passing on in its
    turn,
With faces turn'd sideways or backward towards me to
    listen,
With eyes retrospective towards me.

3

Americanos! conquerors! marches humanitarian!
Foremost! century marches! Libertad! masses!
For you a programme of chants.

Chants of the prairies,
Chants of the long-running Mississippi, and down to the
    Mexican sea,
Chants of Ohio, Indiana, Illinois, Iowa, Wisconsin and
    Minnesota,
Chants going forth from the centre from Kansas, and
    thence equidistant,
Shooting in pulses of fire ceaseless to vivify all.

4

Take my leaves America, take them South and take them
    North,
Make welcome for them everywhere, for they are your own
    offspring,
Surround them East and West, for they would surround
    you,
And you precedents, connect lovingly with them, for they
    connect lovingly with you.

I conn'd old times,
I sat studying at the feet of the great masters,
Now if eligible O that the great masters might return and
study me.

In the name of these States shall I scorn the antique?
Why these are the children of the antique to justify it.

5

Dead poets, philosophs, priests,
Martyrs, artists, inventors, governments long since,
Language-shapers on other shores,
Nations once powerful, now reduced, withdrawn, or
    desolate,

I dare not proceed till I respectfully credit what you have
   left wafted hither,
I have perused it, own it is admirable, (moving awhile
   among it,)
Think nothing can ever be greater, nothing can ever
   deserve more than it deserves,
Regarding it all intently a long while, then dismissing it,
I stand in my place with my own day here.

Here lands female and male,
Here the heir-ship and heiress-ship of the world, here the
   flame of materials,
Here spirituality the translatress, the openly-avow'd,
The ever-tending, the finale of visible forms,
The satisfier, after due long-waiting now advancing,
Yes here comes my mistress the soul.

6

The soul,
Forever and forever – longer than soil is brown and solid –
   longer than water ebbs and flows.

I will make the poems of materials, for I think they are to
   be the most spiritual poems,
And I will make the poems of my body and of mortality,
For I think I shall then supply myself with the poems of
   my soul and of immortality.

I will make a song for these States that no one State may
   under any circumstances be subjected to another State,
And I will make a song that there shall be comity by day
   and by night between all the States, and between any
   two of them,

And I will make a song for the ears of the President, full of
    weapons with menacing points,
And behind the weapons countless dissatisfied faces;
And a song make I of the One form'd out of all,
The fang'd and glittering One whose head is over all,
Resolute warlike One including and over all,
(However high the head of any else that head is over all.)

I will acknowledge contemporary lands,
I will trail the whole geography of the globe and salute
    courteously every city large and small,
And employments! I will put in my poems that with you is
    heroism upon land and sea,
And I will report all heroism from an American point of
    view.

I will sing the song of companionship,
I will show what alone must finally compact these,
I believe these are to found their own ideal of manly love,
    indicating it in me,
I will therefore let flame from me the burning fires that
    were threatening to consume me,
I will lift what has too long kept down those smouldering
    fires,
I will give them complete abandonment,
I will write the evangel-poem of comrades and of love,
For who but I should understand love with all its sorrow
    and joy?
And who but I should be the poet of comrades?

7

I am the credulous man of qualities, ages, races,
I advance from the people in their own spirit,
Here is what sings unrestricted faith.

Omnes! omnes! let others ignore what they may,
I make the poem of evil also, I commemorate that part
    also,
I am myself just as much evil as good, and my nation is –
    I say there is in fact no evil,
(Or if there is I say it is just as important to you, to the
    land or to me, as any thing else.)

I too, following many and follow'd by many, inaugurate a
    religion, I descend into the arena,
(It may be I am destin'd to utter the loudest cries there,
    the winner's pealing shouts,
Who knows? they may rise from me yet, and soar above
    every thing.)

Each is not for its own sake,
I say the whole earth and all the stars in the sky are for
    religion's sake.

I say no man has ever yet been half devout enough,
None has ever yet adored or worship'd half enough,
None has begun to think how divine he himself is, and
    how certain the future is.

I say that the real and permanent grandeur of these States
    must be their religion,
Otherwise there is no real and permanent grandeur;
(Nor character nor life worthy the name without religion,
Nor land nor man or woman without religion.)

8

What are you doing young man?
Are you so earnest, so given up to literature, science, art,
  amours?
These ostensible realities, politics, points?
Your ambition or business whatever it may be?

It is well – against such I say not a word, I am their poet
  also,
But behold! such swiftly subside, burnt up for religion's
  sake,
For not all matter is fuel to heat, impalpable flame, the
  essential life of the earth,
Any more than such are to religion.

9

What do you seek so pensive and silent?
What do you need camerado?
Dear son do you think it is love?

Listen dear son – listen America, daughter or son,
It is a painful thing to love a man or woman to excess,
  and yet it satisfies, it is great,
But there is something else very great, it makes the whole
  coincide,
It, magnificent, beyond materials, with continuous hands
  sweeps and provides for all.

10

Know you, solely to drop in the earth the germs of a
  greater religion,
The following chants each for its kind I sing.

My comrade!
For you to share with me two greatnesses, and a third one
    rising inclusive and more resplendent,
The greatness of Love and Democracy, and the greatness
    of Religion.

Melange mine own, the unseen and the seen,
Mysterious ocean where the streams empty,
Prophetic spirit of materials shifting and flickering around
    me,
Living beings, identities now doubtless near us in the air
    that we know not of,
Contact daily and hourly that will not release me,
These selecting, these in hints demanded of me.

Not he with a daily kiss onward from childhood kissing me,
Has winded and twisted around me that which holds me to
    him,
Any more than I am held to the heavens and all the
    spiritual world,
After what they have done to me, suggesting themes.

O such themes – equalities! O divine average!
Warblings under the sun, usher'd as now, or at noon, or
    setting,
Strains musical flowing through age, now reaching hither,
I take to your reckless and composite chords, add to them,
    and cheerfully pass them forward.

11

As I have walk'd in Alabama my morning walk,
I have seen where the she-bird the mocking-bird sat on her
    nest in the briers hatching her brood.

I have seen the he-bird also,
I have paus'd to hear him near at hand inflating his throat
and joyfully singing.

And while I paus'd it came to me that what he really sang
for was not there only,
Nor for his mate nor himself only, nor all sent back by the
echoes,
But subtle, clandestine, away beyond,
A charge transmitted and gift occult for those being born.

12

Democracy! near at hand to you a throat is now inflating
itself and joyfully singing.

Ma femme! for the brood beyond us and of us,
For those who belong here and those to come,
I exultant to be ready for them will now shake our carols
stronger and haughtier than have ever yet been heard
upon earth.

I will make the songs of passion to give them their way,
And your songs outlaw'd offenders, for I scan you with
kindred eyes, and carry you with me the same as any.

I will make the true poem of riches,
To earn for the body and the mind whatever adheres and
goes forward and is not dropt by death;
I will effuse egotism and show it underlying all, and I will
be the bard of personality,
And I will show of male and female that either is but the
the equal of the other,
And sexual organs and acts! do you concentrate in me, for
I am determin'd to tell you with courageous clear voice
to prove you illustrious,

And I will show that there is no imperfection in the
    present, and can be none in the future,
And I will show that whatever happens to anybody it may
    be turn'd to beautiful results,
And I will show that nothing can happen more beautiful
    than death,
And I will thread a thread through my poems that time
    and events are compact,
And that all the things of the universe are perfect miracles,
    each as profound as any.

I will not make poems with reference to parts,
But I will make poems, songs, thoughts, with reference to
    ensemble,
And I will not sing with reference to a day, but with
    reference to all days,
And I will not make a poem nor the least part of a poem
    but has reference to the soul,
Because having look'd at the objects of the universe, I find
    there is no one nor any particle of one but has reference
    to the soul.

13

Was somebody asking to see the soul?
See, your own shape and countenance, persons, substances,
    beasts, the trees, the running rivers, the rocks and sands.

All hold spiritual joys and afterwards loosen them;
How can the real body ever die and be buried?

Of your real body and any man's or woman's real body,
Item for item it will elude the hands of the corpse-cleaners
    and pass to fitting spheres,
Carrying what has accrued to it from the moment of birth
    to the moment of death.

Not the types set up by the printer return their impression,
  the meaning, the main concern,
Any more than a man's substance and life or a woman's
  substance and life return in the body and the soul,
Indifferently before death and after death.

Behold, the body includes and is the meaning, the main
  concern, and includes and is the soul;
Whoever you are, how superb and how divine is your
  body, or any part of it!

14

Whoever you are, to you endless announcements!

Daughter of the lands did you wait for your poet?
Did you wait for one with a flowing mouth and indicative
  hand?
Toward the male of the States, and toward the female of
  the States,
Exulting words, words to Democracy's lands.

Interlink'd, food-yielding lands!
Land of coal and iron! land of gold! land of cotton, sugar,
  rice!
Land of wheat, beef, pork! land of wool and hemp! land
  of the apple and the grape!
Land of the pastoral plains, the grass-fields of the world!
  land of those sweet-air'd interminable plateaus!
Land of the herd, the garden, the healthy house of adobie!
Lands where the north-west Columbia winds, and where
  the south-west Colorado winds!
Land of the eastern Chesapeake! land of the Delaware!
Land of Ontario, Erie, Huron, Michigan!

Land of the Old Thirteen! Massachusetts land! land of
    Vermont and Connecticut!
Land of the ocean shores! land of sierras and peaks!
Land of boatmen and sailors! fishermen's land!
Inextricable lands! the clutch'd together! the passionate
    ones!
The side by side! the elder and younger brothers! the
    bony-limb'd!
The great women's land! the feminine! the experienced
    sisters and the inexperienced sisters!
Far breath'd land! Arctic braced! Mexican breez'd! the
    diverse! the compact!
The Pennsylvanian! the Virginian! the double Carolinian!
O all and each well-loved by me! my intrepid nations! O I
    at any rate include you all with perfect love!
I cannot be discharged from you! not from one any sooner
    than another!
O death! O for all that, I am yet of you unseen this hour
    with irrepressible love,
Walking New England, a friend, a traveler,
Splashing my bare feet in the edge of the summer ripples
    on Paumanok's sands,
Crossing the prairies, dwelling again in Chicago, dwelling
    in every town,
Observing shows, births, improvements, structures, arts,
Listening to orators and oratresses in public halls,
Of and through the States as during life, each man and
    woman my neighbor,
The Louisianian, the Georgian, as near to me, and I as near
    to him and her,
The Mississippian and Arkansian yet with me, and I yet
    with any of them,
Yet upon the plains west of the spinal river, yet in my
    house of adobie,

Yet returning eastward, yet in the Seaside State or in
    Maryland,
Yet Kanadian cheerily braving the winter, the snow and
    ice welcome to me,
Yet a true son either of Maine or of the Granite State,
    or the Narragansett Bay State, or the Empire State,
Yet sailing to other shores to annex the same, yet
    welcoming every new brother,
Hereby applying these leaves to the new ones from the
    hour they unite with the old ones,
Coming among the new ones myself to be their companion
    and equal, coming personally to you now,
Enjoining you to acts, characters, spectacles, with me.

15

With me with firm holding, yet haste, haste on.

For your life adhere to me,
(I may have to be persuaded many times before I consent
    to give myself really to you, but what of that?
Must not Nature be persuaded many times?)

No dainty dolce affettuoso I,
Bearded, sun-burnt, gray-neck'd, forbidding, I have
    arrived,
To be wrestled with as I pass for the solid prizes of the
    universe,
For such I afford whoever can persevere to win them.

16

On my way a moment I pause,
Here for you! and here for America!
Still the present I raise aloft, still the future of the States
    I harbinge glad and sublime,
And for the past I pronounce what the air holds of the
    red aborigines.

The red aborigines,
Leaving natural breaths, sounds of rain and winds, calls
    as of birds and animals in the woods, syllabled to us for
    names,
Okonee, Koosa, Ottawa, Monongahela, Sauk, Natchez,
    Chattahoochee, Kaqueta, Oronoco,
Wabash, Miami, Saginaw, Chippewa, Oshkosh,
    Walla-Walla,
Leaving such to the States they melt, they depart, charging
    the water and the land with names.

17

Expanding and swift, henceforth,
Elements, breeds, adjustments, turbulent, quick and
    audacious,
A world primal again, vistas of glory incessant and
    branching,
A new race dominating previous ones and grander far,
    with new contests,
New politics, new literatures and religions, new inventions
    and arts.

These, my voice announcing – I will sleep no more but
    arise,
You oceans that have been calm within me! how I feel you,
    fathomless, stirring, preparing unprecedented waves
    and storms.

18

See, steamers steaming through my poems,
See, in my poems immigrants continually coming and
    landing,
See, in arriere, the wigwam, the trail, the hunter's hut,
    the flat-boat, the maize-leaf, the claim, the rude fence,
    and the backwoods village,
See, on the one side the Western Sea and on the other the
    Eastern Sea, how they advance and retreat upon my
    poems as upon their own shores,
See, pastures and forests in my poems – see, animals wild
    and tame – see, beyond the Kaw, countless herds of
    buffalo feeding on short curly grass,
See, in my poems, cities, solid, vast, inland, with paved
    streets, with iron and stone edifices, ceaseless vehicles,
    and commerce,
See, the many-cylinder'd steam printing-press – see, the
    electric telegraph stretching across the continent,
See, through Atlantica's depths pulses American Europe
    reaching, pulses of Europe duly return'd,
See, the strong and quick locomotive as it departs, panting,
    blowing the steam-whistle,
See, ploughmen ploughing farms – see, miners digging
    mines – see, the numberless factories,
See, mechanics busy at their benches with tools – see from
    among them superior judges, philosophs, Presidents,
    emerge, drest in working dresses,

See, lounging through the shops and fields of the States,
    me well-belov'd, close-held by day and night,
Here the loud echoes of my songs there – read the hints
    come at last.

19

O camerado close! O you and me at last, and us two only.
O a word to clear one's path ahead endlessly!
O something ecstatic and undemonstrable! O music wild!
O now I triumph – and you shall also;
O hand in hand – O wholesome pleasure – O one more
    desirer and lover!
O to haste firm holding – to haste, haste on with me.

1856

Song of Myself

1

I celebrate myself, and sing myself,
And what I assume you shall assume,
For every atom belonging to me as good belongs to you.

I loafe and invite my soul,
I lean and loafe at my ease observing a spear of summer
  grass.

My tongue, every atom of my blood, form'd from this
  soil, this air,
Born here of parents born here from parents the same,
  and their parents the same,
I, now thirty-seven years old in perfect health begin,
Hoping to cease not till death.

Creeds and schools in abeyance,
Retiring back a while suffced at what they are, but never
  forgotten,
I harbor for good or bad, I permit to speak at every
  hazard,
Nature without check with original energy.

2

Houses and rooms are full of perfumes, the shelves are
  crowded with perfumes,
I breathe the fragrance myself and know it and like it,
The distillation would intoxicate me also, but I shall not
  let it.

The atmosphere is not a perfume, it has no taste of the
    distillation, it is odorless,
It is for my mouth forever, I am in love with it,
I will go to the bank by the wood and become undisguised
    and naked,
I am mad for it to be in contact with me.

The smoke of my own breath,
Echoes, ripples, buzz'd whispers, love-root, silk-thread,
    crotch and vine,
My respiration and inspiration, the beating of my heart,
    the passing of blood and air through my lungs,
The sniff of green leaves and dry leaves, and of the shore
    and dark-color'd sea-rocks, and of hay in the barn,
The sound of the belch'd words of my voice loos'd to the
    eddies of the wind,
A few light kisses, a few embraces, a reaching around of
    arms,
The play of shine and shade on the trees as the supple
    boughs wag,
The delight alone or in the rush of the streets, or along
    the fields and hill-sides,
The feeling of health, the full-noon trill, the song of me
    rising from bed and meeting the sun.

Have you reckon'd a thousand acres much? have you
    reckon'd the earth much?
Have you practis'd so long to learn to read?
Have you felt so proud to get at the meaning of poems?

Stop this day and night with me and you shall possess the
    origin of all poems,
You shall possess the good of the earth and sun, (there are
    millions of suns left,)

You shall no longer take things at second or third hand,
    nor look through the eyes of the dead, nor feed on the
    spectres in books,
You shall not look through my eyes either, nor take things
    from me,
You shall listen to all sides and filter them from your self.

3

I have heard what the talkers were talking, the talk of the
    beginning and the end,
But I do not talk of the beginning or the end.

There was never any more inception than there is now,
Nor any more youth or age than there is now,
And will never be any more perfection than there is now,
Nor any more heaven or hell than there is now.

Urge and urge and urge,
Always the procreant urge of the world.

Out of the dimness opposite equals advance, always
    substance and increase, always sex,
Always a knit of identity, always distinction, always a breed
    of life.

To elaborate is no avail, learn'd and unlearn'd feel that
    it is so.

Sure as the most certain sure, plumb in the uprights, well
    entretied, braced in the beams,
Stout as a horse, affectionate, haughty, electrical,
I and this mystery here we stand.

Clear and sweet is my soul, and clear and sweet is all that
   is not my soul.

Lack one lacks both, and the unseen is proved by the seen,
Till that becomes unseen and receives proof in its turn.

Showing the best and dividing it from the worst age vexes
   age,
Knowing the perfect fitness and equanimity of things,
   while they discuss I am silent, and go bathe and admire
   myself.

Welcome is every organ and attribute of me, and of any
   man hearty and clean,
Not an inch nor a particle of an inch is vile, and none
   shall be less familiar than the rest.

I am satisfied – I see, dance, laugh, sing;
As the hugging and loving bed-fellow sleeps at my side
   through the night, and withdraws at the peep of the day
   with stealthy tread,
Leaving me baskets cover'd with white towels swelling the
   house with their plenty,
Shall I postpone my acceptation and realization and scream
   at my eyes,
That they turn from gazing after and down the road,
And forthwith cipher and show me to a cent,
Exactly the value of one and exactly the value of two, and
   which is ahead?

4

Trippers and askers surround me,
People I meet, the effect upon me of my early life or the
   ward and city I live in, or the nation,

The latest dates, discoveries, inventions, societies, authors
    old and new,
My dinner, dress, associates, looks, compliments, dues,
The real or fancied indifference of some man or woman I
    love,
The sickness of one of my folks or of myself, or ill-doing
    or loss or lack of money, or depressions or exaltations,
Battles, the horrors of fratricidal war, the fever of doubtful
    news, the fitful events;
These come to me days and nights and go from me again,
But they are not the Me myself.

Apart from the pulling and hauling stands what I am,
Stands amused, complacent, compassionating, idle, unitary,
Looks down, is erect, or bends an arm on an impalpable
    certain rest,
Looking with side-curved head curious what will come
    next,
Both in and out of the game and watching and wondering
    at it.

Backward I see in my own days where I sweated through
    fog with linguists and contenders,
I have no mockings or arguments, I witness and wait.

5

I believe in you my soul, the other I am must not abase
    itself to you,
And you must not be abased to the other.

Loafe with me on the grass, loose the stop from your
    throat,
Not words, not music or rhyme I want, not custom or
    lecture, not even the best,
Only the lull I like, the hum of your valvèd voice.

I mind how once we lay such a transparent summer
  morning,
How you settled your head athwart my hips and gently
  turn'd over upon me,
And parted the shirt from my bosom-bone, and plunged
  your tongue to my bare-stript heart,
And reach'd till you felt my beard, and reach'd till you
  held my feet.

Swiftly arose and spread around me the peace and
  knowledge that pass all the argument of the earth,
And I know that the hand of God is the promise of my
  own,
And I know that the spirit of God is the brother of my
  own,
And that all the men ever born are also my brothers, and
  the women my sisters and lovers,
And that a kelson of the creation is love,
And limitless are leaves stiff or drooping in the fields,
And brown ants in the little wells beneath them,
And mossy scabs of the worm fence, heap'd stones, elder,
  mullein and poke-weed.

6

A child said *What is the grass?* fetching it to me with full
  hands;
How could I answer the child? I do not know what it is
  any more than he.

I guess it must be the flag of my disposition, out of hopeful
  green stuff woven.

Or I guess it is the handkerchief of the Lord,
A scented gift and remembrancer designedly dropt,
Bearing the owner's name someway in the corners, that we
    may see and remark, and say *Whose?*

Or I guess the grass is itself a child, the produced babe
    of the vegetation.

Or I guess it is a uniform hieroglyphic,
And it means, Sprouting alike in broad zones and narrow
    zones,
Growing among black folks as among white,
Kanuck, Tuckahoe, Congressman, Cuff, I give them the
    same, I receive them the same.

And now it seems to me the beautiful uncut hair of graves.

Tenderly will I use you curling grass,
It may be you transpire from the breasts of young men,
It may be if I had known them I would have loved them,
It may be you are from old people, or from offspring taken
    soon out of their mothers' laps,
And here you are the mothers' laps.

This grass is very dark to be from the white heads of old
    mothers,
Darker than the colorless beards of old men,
Dark to come from under the faint red roofs of mouths.

O I perceive after all so many uttering tongues,
And I perceive they do not come from the roofs of mouths
    for nothing.

I wish I could translate the hints about the dead young
    men and women,
And the hints about old men and mothers, and the
    offspring taken soon out of their laps.

What do you think has become of the young and old men?
And what do you think has become of the women and
    children?

They are alive and well somewhere,
The smallest sprout shows there is really no death,
And if ever there was it led forward life, and does not wait
    at the end to arrest it,
And ceas'd the moment life appear'd.

All goes onward and outward, nothing collapses,
And to die is different from what any one supposed, and
    luckier.

7

Has any one supposed it lucky to be born?
I hasten to inform him or her it is just as lucky to die, and
    I know it.

I pass death with the dying and birth with the new-wash'd
    babe, and am not contain'd between my hat and boots,
And peruse manifold objects, no two alike and every one
    good,
The earth good and the stars good, and their adjuncts all
    good.

I am not an earth nor an adjunct of an earth,
I am the mate and companion of people, all just as
    immortal and fathomless as myself,
(They do not know how immortal, but I know.)

Every kind for itself and its own, for me mine male and
    female,
For me those that have been boys and that love women,
For me the man that is proud and feels how it stings to be
    slighted,
For me the sweet-heart and the old maid, for me mothers
    and the mothers of mothers,
For me lips that have smiled, eyes that have shed tears,
For me children and the begetters of children.

Undrape! you are not guilty to me, nor stale nor discarded,
I see through the broadcloth and gingham whether or no,
And am around, tenacious, acquisitive, tireless, and cannot
    be shaken away.

8

The little one sleeps in its cradle,
I lift the gauze and look a long time, and silently brush
    away flies with my hand.
The youngster and the red-faced girl turn aside up the
    busy hill,
I peeringly view them from the top.

The suicide sprawls on the bloody floor of the bedroom,
I witness the corpse with its dabbled hair, I note where the
    pistol has fallen.

The blab of the pave, tires of carts, sluff of boot-soles, talk
    of the promenaders,
The heavy omnibus, the driver with his interrogating
    thumb, the clank of the shod horses on the granite floor,
The snow-sleighs, clinking, shouted jokes, pelts of
    snow-balls,

The hurrahs for popular favorites, the fury of rous'd
    mobs,
The flap of the curtain'd litter, a sick man inside borne
    to the hospital,
The meeting of enemies, the sudden oath, the blows and
    fall,
The excited crowd, the policeman with his star quickly
    working his passage to the centre of the crowd,
The impassive stones that receive and return so many
    echoes,
What groans of over-fed or half-starv'd who fall sunstruck
    or in fits,
What exclamations of women taken suddenly who hurry
    home and give birth to babes,
What living and buried speech is always vibrating here,
    what howls restrain'd by decorum,
Arrests of criminals, slights, adulterous offers made,
    acceptances, rejections with convex lips,
I mind them or the show or resonance of them – I come
    and I depart.

9

The big doors of the country barn stand open and ready,
The dried grass of the harvest-time loads the slow-drawn
    wagon,
The clear light plays on the brown gray and green
    intertinged,
The armfuls are pack'd to the sagging mow.

I am there, I help, I came stretch'd atop of the load,
I felt its soft jolts, one leg reclined on the other,
I jump from the cross-beams and seize the clover and
    timothy,
And roll head over heels and tangle my hair full of wisps.

10

Alone far in the wilds and mountains I hunt,
Wandering amazed at my own lightness and glee,
In the late afternoon choosing a safe spot to pass the night,
Kindling a fire and broiling the fresh-kill'd game,
Falling asleep on the gather'd leaves with my dog and gun
    by my side.

The Yankee clipper is under her sky-sails, she cuts the
    sparkle and scud,
My eyes settle the land, I bend at her prow or shout
    joyously from the deck.

The boatmen and clam-diggers arose early and stopt for
    me,
I tuck'd my trowser-ends in my boots and went and had
    a good time;
You should have been with us that day round the
    chowder-kettle.

I saw the marriage of the trapper in the open air in the
    far west, the bride was a red girl,
Her father and his friends sat near cross-legged and
    dumbly smoking, they had moccasins to their feet and
    large thick blankets hanging from their shoulders,
On a bank lounged the trapper, he was drest mostly in
    skins, his luxuriant beard and curls protected his neck,
    he held his bride by the hand.
She had long eyelashes, her head was bare, her coarse
    straight locks descended upon her voluptuous limbs and
    reach'd to her feet.

The runaway slave came to my house and stopt outside,
I heard his motions crackling the twigs of the woodpile,
Through the swung half-door of the kitchen I saw him
    limpsy and weak,
And went where he sat on a log and led him in and assured
    him,
And brought water and fill'd a tub for his sweated body
    and bruis'd feet,
And gave him a room that enter'd from my own, and gave
    him some coarse clean clothes,
And remember perfectly well his revolving eyes and his
    awkwardness,
And remember putting plasters on the galls of his neck
    and ankles;
He staid with me a week before he was recuperated and
    pass'd north,
I had him sit next me at table, my fire-lock lean'd in the
    corner.

11

Twenty-eight young men bathe by the shore,
Twenty-eight young men and all so friendly;
Twenty-eight years of womanly life and all so lonesome.

She owns the fine house by the rise of the bank,
She hides handsome and richly drest aft the blinds of the
    window.

Which of the young men does she like the best?
Ah the homeliest of them is beautiful to her.

Where are you off to, lady? for I see you,
You splash in the water there, yet stay stock still in your
    room.

Dancing and laughing along the beach came the
   twenty-ninth bather,
The rest did not see her, but she saw them and loved
   them.

The beards of the young men glisten'd with wet, it ran
   from their long hair,
Little streams pass'd all over their bodies.

An unseen hand also pass'd over their bodies,
It descended tremblingly from their temples and ribs.

The young men float on their backs, their white bellies
   bulge to the sun, they do not ask who seizes fast to
   them,
They do not know who puffs and declines with pendant
   and bending arch,
They do not think whom they souse with spray.

12

The butcher-boy puts off his killing-clothes, or sharpens
   his knife at the stall in the market,
I loiter enjoying his repartee and his shuffle and
   break-down.

Blacksmiths with grimed and hairy chests environ the
   anvil,
Each has his main-sledge, they are all out, there is a great
   heat in the fire.

From the cinder-strew'd threshold I follow their
   movements,
The lithe sheer of their waists plays even with their
   massive arms,

Overhand the hammers swing, overhand so slow, overhand
    so sure,
They do not hasten, each man hits in his place.

13

The negro holds firmly the reins of his four horses, the
    block swags underneath on its tied-over chain,
The negro that drives the long dray of the stone-yard,
    steady and tall he stands pois'd on one leg on the
    string-piece,
His blue shirt exposes his ample neck and breast and
    loosens over his hip-band,
His glance is calm and commanding, he tosses the slouch
    of his hat away from his forehead,
The sun falls on his crispy hair and mustache, falls on the
    black of his polish'd and perfect limbs.

I behold the picturesque giant and love him, and I do not
    stop there,
I go with the team also.

In me the caresser of life wherever moving, backward as
    well as forward sluing,
To niches aside and junior bending, not a person or object
    missing,
Absorbing all to myself and for this song.

Oxen that rattle the yoke and chain or halt in the leafy
    shade, what is that you express in your eyes?
It seems to me more than all the print I have read in my
    life.

My tread scares the wood-drake and wood-duck on my
    distant and day-long ramble,
They rise together, they slowly circle around.

I believe in those wing'd purposes,
And acknowledge red, yellow, white, playing within me,
And consider green and violet and the tufted crown
     intentional,
And do not call the tortoise unworthy because she is not
     something else,
And the jay in the woods never studied the gamut, yet
     trills pretty well to me,
And the look of the bay mare shames silliness out of me.

14

The wild gander leads his flock through the cool night,
Ya-honk he says, and sounds it down to me like an
     invitation,
The pert may suppose it meaningless, but I listening close,
Find its purpose and place up there toward the wintry sky.

The sharp-hoof'd moose of the north, the cat on the
     house-sill, the chickadee, the prairie-dog,
The litter of the grunting sow as they tug at her teats,
The brood of the turkey-hen and she with her half-spread
     wings,
I see in them and myself the same old law.

The press of my foot to the earth springs a hundred
     affections,
They scorn the best I can do to relate them.

I am enamour'd of growing out-doors,
Of men that live among cattle or taste of the ocean or
     woods,
Of the builders and steerers of ships and the wielders of
     axes and mauls, and the drivers of horses,
I can eat and sleep with them week in and week out.

What is commonest, cheapest, nearest, easiest, is Me,
Me going in for my chances, spending for vast returns,
Adorning myself to bestow myself on the first that will
    take me,
Not asking the sky to come down to my good will,
Scattering it freely forever.

15

The pure contralto sings in the organ loft,
The carpenter dresses his plank, the tongue of his
    foreplane whistles its wild ascending lisp,
The married and unmarried children ride home to their
    Thanksgiving dinner,
The pilot seizes the king-pin, he heaves down with a
    strong arm,
The mate stands braced in the whale-boat, lance and
    harpoon are ready,
The duck-shooter walks by silent and cautious stretches,
The deacons are ordain'd with cross'd hands at the altar,
The spinning-girl retreats and advances to the hum of
    the big wheel,
The farmer stops by the bars as he walks on a First-day
    loafe and looks at the oats and rye,
The lunatic is carried at last to the asylum a confirm'd
    case,
(He will never sleep any more as he did in the cot in his
    mother's bed-room;)
The jour printer with gray head and gaunt jaws works at
    his case,
He turns his quid of tobacco while his eyes blurr with
    the manuscript;
The malform'd limbs are tied to the surgeon's table,
What is removed drops horribly in a pail;

The quadroon girl is sold at the auction-stand, the
    drunkard nods by the bar-room stove,
The machinist rolls up his sleeves, the policeman travels
    his beat, the gate-keeper marks who pass,
The young fellow drives the express-wagon, (I love him,
    though I do not know him;)
The half-breed straps on his light boots to compete in
    the race,
The western turkey-shooting draws old and young, some
    lean on their rifles, some sit on logs,
Out from the crowd steps the marksman, takes his
    position, levels his piece;
The groups of newly-come immigrants cover the wharf
    or levee,
As the woolly-pates hoe in the sugar-field, the overseer
    views them from his saddle,
The bugle calls in the ball-room, the gentlemen run for
    their partners, the dancers bow to each other,
The youth lies awake in the cedar-roof'd garret and harks
    to the musical rain,
The Wolverine sets traps on the creek that helps fill the
    Huron,
The squaw wrapt in her yellow-hemm'd cloth is offering
    moccasins and bead-bags for sale,
The connoisseur peers along the exhibition-gallery with
    half-shut eyes bent sideways,
As the deck-hands make fast the steamboat the plank is
    thrown for the shore-going passengers,
The young sister holds out the skein while the elder sister
    winds it off in a ball, and stops now and then for the
    knots,
The one-year wife is recovering and happy having a week
    ago borne her first child,

The clean-hair'd Yankee girl works with her
  sewing-machine or in the factory or mill,
The paving-man leans on his two-handed rammer, the
  reporter's lead flies swiftly over the note-book, the
  sign-painter is lettering with blue and gold,
The canal boy trots on the tow-path, the book-keeper
  counts at his desk, the shoemaker waxes his thread,
The conductor beats time for the band and all the
  performers follow him,
The child is baptized, the convert is making his first
  professions,
The regatta is spread on the bay, the race is begun, (how
  the white sails sparkle!)
The drover watching his drove sings out to them that
  would stray,
The pedler sweats with his pack on his back, (the
  purchaser higgling about the odd cent;)
The bride unrumples her white dress, the minute-hand
  of the clock moves slowly,
The opium-eater reclines with rigid head and just-open'd
  lips,
The prostitute draggles her shawl, her bonnet bobs on
  her tipsy and pimpled neck,
The crowd laugh at her blackguard oaths, the men jeer
  and wink to each other,
(Miserable! I do not laugh at your oaths nor jeer you;)
The President holding a cabinet council is surrounded by
  the great Secretaries,
On the piazza walk three matrons stately and friendly with
  twined arms,
The crew of the fish-smack pack repeated layers of halibut
  in the hold,
The Missourian crosses the plains toting his wares and his
  cattle,

As the fare-collector goes through the train he gives notice
    by the jingling of loose change,
The floor-men are laying the floor, the tinners are tinning
    the roof, the masons are calling for mortar,
In single file each shouldering his hod pass onward the
    laborers;
Seasons pursuing each other the indescribable crowd is
    gather'd, it is the fourth of Seventh-month, (what
    salutes of cannon and small arms!)
Seasons pursuing each other the plougher ploughs, the
    mower mows, and the winter-grain falls in the ground;
Off on the lakes the pike-fisher watches and waits by the
    hole in the frozen surface,
The stumps stand thick round the clearing, the squatter
    strikes deep with his axe,
Flatboatmen make fast towards dusk near the cotton-wood
    or pecan-trees,
Coon-seekers go through the regions of the Red river or
    through those drain'd by the Tennessee, or through
    those of the Arkansas,
Torches shine in the dark that hangs on the Chattahooche
    or Altamahaw,
Patriarchs sit at supper with sons and grandsons and
    great-grandsons around them,
In walls of adobie, in canvas tents, rest hunters and
    trappers after their day's sport,
The city sleeps and the country sleeps,
The living sleep for their time, the dead sleep for their
    time,
The old husband sleeps by his wife and the young husband
    sleeps by his wife;
And these tend inward to me, and I tend outward to them,
And such as it is to be of these more or less I am,
And of these one and all I weave the song of myself.

16

I am of old and young, of the foolish as much as the wise,
Regardless of others, ever regardful of others,
Maternal as well as paternal, a child as well as a man,
Stuff'd with the stuff that is coarse and stuff'd with the
     stuff that is fine,
One of the Nation of many nations, the smallest the same
     and the largest the same,
A Southerner soon as a Northerner, a planter nonchalant
     and hospitable down by the Oconee I live,
A Yankee bound my own way ready for trade, my joints
     the limberest joints on earth and the sternest joints on
     earth,
A Kentuckian walking the vale of the Elkhorn in my
     deer-skin leggings, a Louisianian or Georgian,
A boatman over lakes or bays or along coasts, a Hoosier,
     Badger, Buckeye;
At home on Kanadian snow-shoes or up in the bush, or
     with fishermen off Newfoundland,
At home in the fleet of ice-boats, sailing with the rest and
     tacking,
At home on the hills of Vermont or in the woods of Maine,
     or the Texan ranch,
Comrade of Californians, comrade of free
     North-Westerners, (loving their big proportions,)
Comrade of raftsmen and coalmen, comrade of all who
     shake hands and welcome to drink and meat,
A learner with the simplest, a teacher of the thoughtfullest,
A novice beginning yet experient of myriads of seasons,
Of every hue and caste am I, of every rank and religion,
A farmer, mechanic, artist, gentleman, sailor, quaker,
Prisoner, fancy-man, rowdy, lawyer, physician, priest.

I resist any thing better than my own diversity,
Breathe the air but leave plenty after me,
And am not stuck up, and am in my place.

(The moth and the fish-eggs are in their place,
The bright suns I see and the dark suns I cannot see are
   in their place,
The palpable is in its place and the impalpable is in its
   place.)

17

These are really the thoughts of all men in all ages and
   lands, they are not original with me,
If they are not yours as much as mine they are nothing, or
   next to nothing,
If they are not the riddle and the untying of the riddle
   they are nothing,
If they are not just as close as they are distant they are
   nothing.

This is the grass that grows wherever the land is and the
   water is,
This the common air that bathes the globe.

18

With music strong I come, with my cornets and my
   drums,
I play not marches for accepted victors only, I play marches
   for conquer'd and slain persons.

Have you heard that it was good to gain the day?
I also say it is good to fall, battles are lost in the same
   spirit in which they are won.

I beat and pound for the dead,
I blow through my embouchures my loudest and gayest
    for them.

Vivas to those who have fail'd!
And to those whose war-vessels sank in the sea!
And to those themselves who sank in the sea!
And to all generals that lost engagements, and all overcome
    heroes!
And the numberless unknown heroes equal to the greatest
    heroes known!

19

This is the meal equally set, this the meat for natural
    hunger,
It is for the wicked just the same as the righteous, I make
    appointments with all,
I will not have a single person slighted or left away,
The kept-woman, sponger, thief, are hereby invited,
The heavy-lipp'd slave is invited, the venerealee is invited;
There shall be no difference between them and the rest.

This is the press of a bashful hand, this the float and
    odor of hair,
This the touch of my lips to yours, this the murmur of
    yearning,
This the far-off depth and height reflecting my own face,
This the thoughtful merge of myself, and the outlet again.

Do you guess I have some intricate purpose?
Well I have, for the Fourth-month showers have, and the
    mica on the side of a rock has.

Do you take it I would astonish?
Does the daylight astonish? does the early redstart
   twittering through the woods?
Do I astonish more than they?

This hour I tell things in confidence,
I might not tell everybody, but I will tell you.

20

Who goes there? hankering, gross, mystical, nude;
How is it I extract strength from the beef I eat?

What is a man anyhow? what am I? what are you?

All I mark as my own you shall offset it with your own,
Else it were time lost listening to me.

I do not snivel that snivel the world over,
That months are vacuums and the ground but wallow
   and filth.

Whimpering and truckling fold with powders for invalids,
   conformity, goes to the fourth-remov'd,
I wear my hat as I please indoors or out.

Why should I pray? why should I venerate and be
   ceremonious?

Having pried through the strata, analyzed to a hair,
   counsel'd with doctors and calculated close,
I find no sweeter fat than sticks to my own bones.

In all people I see myself, none more and not one a
   barley-corn less,
And the good or bad I say of myself I say of them.

I know I am solid and sound,
To me the converging objects of the universe perpetually
    flow,
All are written to me, and I must get what the writing
    means.

I know I am deathless,
I know this orbit of mine cannot be swept by a carpenter's
    compass,
I know I shall not pass like a child's carlacue cut with a
    burnt stick at night.

I know I am august,
I do not trouble my spirit to vindicate itself or be
    understood,
I see that the elementary laws never apologize,
(I reckon I behave no prouder than the level I plant my
    house by, after all.)

I exist as I am, that is enough,
If no other in the world be aware I sit content,
And if each and all be aware I sit content.

One world is aware and by far the largest to me, and
    that is myself,
And whether I come to my own to-day or in ten thousand
    or ten million years,
I can cheerfully take it now, or with equal cheerfulness
    I can wait.

My foothold is tenon'd and mortis'd in granite,
I laugh at what you call dissolution,
And I know the amplitude of time.

21

I am the poet of the Body and I am the poet of the Soul,
The pleasures of heaven are with me and the pains of
    hell are with me,
The first I graft and increase upon myself, the latter I
    translate into a new tongue.

I am the poet of the woman the same as the man,
And I say it is as great to be a woman as to be a man,
And I say there is nothing greater than the mother of men.

I chant the chant of dilation or pride,
We have had ducking and deprecating about enough,
I show that size is only development.

Have you outstript the rest? are you the President?
It is a trifle, they will more than arrive there every one,
    and still pass on.

I am he that walks with the tender and growing night,
I call to the earth and sea half-held by the night.

Press close bare-bosom'd night – press close magnetic
    nourishing night!
Night of south winds – night of the large few stars!
Still nodding night – mad naked summer night.

Smile O voluptuous cool-breath'd earth!
Earth of the slumbering and liquid trees!
Earth of departed sunset – earth of the mountains
    misty-topt!
Earth of the vitreous pour of the full moon just tinged with
    blue!

Earth of shine and dark mottling the tide of the river!
Earth of the limpid gray of clouds brighter and clearer for
  my sake!
Far-swooping elbow'd earth – rich apple-blossom'd earth!
Smile, for your lover comes.

Prodigal, you have given me love – therefore I to you give
  love!
O unspeakable passionate love.

22

You sea! I resign myself to you also – I guess what you
  mean,
I behold from the beach your crooked inviting fingers,
I believe you refuse to go back without feeling of me,
We must have a turn together, I undress, hurry me out
  of sight of the land,
Cushion me soft, rock me in billowy drowse,
Dash me with amorous wet, I can repay you.

Sea of stretch'd ground-swells,
Sea breathing broad and convulsive breaths,
Sea of the brine of life and of unshovell'd yet
  always-ready graves,
Howler and scooper of storms, capricious and dainty sea,
I am integral with you, I too am of one phase and of all
  phases.

Partaker of influx and efflux I, extoller of hate and
  conciliation,
Extoller of amies and those that sleep in each others' arms.

I am he attesting sympathy,
(Shall I make my list of things in the house and skip the
  house that supports them?)

I am not the poet of goodness only, I do not decline to
    be the poet of wickedness also.

What blurt is this about virtue and about vice?
Evil propels me and reform of evil propels me, I stand
    indifferent,
My gait is no fault-finder's or rejecter's gait,
I moisten the roots of all that has grown.

Did you fear some scrofula out of the unflagging
    pregnancy?
Did you guess the celestial laws are yet to be work'd
    over and rectified?

I find one side a balance and the antipodal side a balance,
Soft doctrine as steady help as stable doctrine,
Thoughts and deeds of the present our rouse and early
    start.

This minute that comes to me over the past decillions,
There is no better than it and now.

What behaved well in the past or behaves well to-day is
    not such a wonder,
The wonder is always and always how there can be a
    mean man or an infidel.

23

Endless unfolding of words of ages!
And mine a word of the modern, the word En-Masse.

A word of the faith that never balks,
Here or henceforward it is all the same to me, I accept
    Time absolutely.

It alone is without flaw, it alone rounds and completes all,
That mystic baffling wonder alone completes all.

I accept Reality and dare not question it,
Materialism first and last imbuing.

Hurray for positive science! long live exact demonstration!
Fetch stonecrop mixt with cedar and branches of lilac,
This is the lexicographer, this the chemist, this made a
    grammar of the old cartouches,
These mariners put the ship through dangerous unknown
    seas,
This is the geologist, this works with the scalpel, and this
    is a mathematician.

Gentlemen, to you the first honors always!
Your facts are useful, and yet they are not my dwelling,
I but enter by them to an area of my dwelling.

Less the reminders of properties told my words,
And more the reminders they of life untold, and of freedom
    and extrication,
And make short account of neuters and geldings, and
    favor men and women fully equipt,
And beat the gong of revolt, and stop with fugitives and
    them that plot and conspire.

24

Walt Whitman, a kosmos, of Manhattan the son,
Turbulent, fleshy, sensual, eating, drinking and breeding,
No sentimentalist, no stander above men and women
    or apart from them,
No more modest than immodest.

Unscrew the locks from the doors!
Unscrew the doors themselves from their jambs!

Whoever degrades another degrades me,
And whatever is done or said returns at last to me.

Through me the afflatus surging and surging, through me
the current and index.

I speak the pass-word primeval, I give the sign of
democracy,
By God! I will accept nothing which all cannot have
their counterpart of on the same terms.

Through me many long dumb voices,
Voices of the interminable generations of prisoners and
slaves,
Voices of the diseas'd and despairing and of thieves and
dwarfs,
Voices of cycles of preparation and accretion,
And of the threads that connect the stars, and of wombs
and of the father-stuff,
And of the rights of them the others are down upon,
Of the deform'd, trivial, flat, foolish, despised,
Fog in the air, beetles rolling balls of dung.

Through me forbidden voices,
Voices of sexes and lusts, voices veil'd and I remove the
veil,
Voices indecent by me clarified and transfigur'd.

I do not press my fingers across my mouth,
I keep as delicate around the bowels as around the head
and heart,
Copulation is no more rank to me than death is.

I believe in the flesh and the appetites,
Seeing, hearing, feeling, are miracles, and each part and
    tag of me is a miracle.

Divine am I inside and out, and I make holy whatever I
    touch or am touch'd from,
The scent of these arm-pits aroma finer than prayer,
This head more than churches, bibles, and all the creeds.

If I worship one thing more than another it shall be the
    spread of my own body, or any part of it,
Translucent mould of me it shall be you!
Shaded ledges and rests it shall be you!
Firm masculine colter it shall be you!
Whatever goes to the tilth of me it shall be you!
You my rich blood! your milky stream pale strippings of
    my life!
Breast that presses against other breasts it shall be you!
My brain it shall be your occult convolutions!
Root of wash'd sweet-flag! timorous pond-snipe! nest of
    guarded duplicate eggs! it shall be you!
Mix'd tussled hay of head, beard, brawn, it shall be you!
Trickling sap of maple, fibre of manly wheat, it shall be
    you!
Sun so generous it shall be you!
Vapors lighting and shading my face it shall be you!
You sweaty brooks and dews it shall be you!
Winds whose soft-tickling genitals rub against me it shall
    be you!
Broad muscular fields, branches of live oak, loving lounger
    in my winding paths, it shall be you!
Hands I have taken, face I have kiss'd, mortal I have ever
    touch'd, it shall be you.

I dote on myself, there is that lot of me and all so luscious,
Each moment and whatever happens thrills me with joy,
I cannot tell how my ankles bend, nor whence the cause
    of my faintest wish,
Nor the cause of the friendship I emit, nor the cause of
    the friendship I take again.

That I walk up my stoop, I pause to consider if it really be,
A morning-glory at my window satisfies me more than the
    metaphysics of books.

To behold the day-break!
The little light fades the immense and diaphanous
    shadows,
The air tastes good to my palate.

Hefts of the moving world at innocent gambols silently
    rising freshly exuding,
Scooting obliquely high and low.

Something I cannot see puts upward libidinous prongs,
Seas of bright juice suffuse heaven.

The earth by the sky staid with, the daily close of their
    junction,
The heav'd challenge from the east that moment over my
    head,
The mocking taunt, See then whether you shall be master!

25

Dazzling and tremendous how quick the sun-rise would
    kill me,
If I could not now and always send sun-rise out of me.

We also ascend dazzling and tremendous as the sun,
We found our own O my soul in the calm and cool of the
    daybreak.

My voice goes after what my eyes cannot reach,
With the twirl of my tongue I encompass worlds and
    volumes of worlds.

Speech is the twin of my vision, it is unequal to measure
    itself,
It provokes me forever, it says sarcastically,
Walt you contain enough, why don't you let it out then?

Come now I will not be tantalized, you conceive too much
    of articulation,
Do you not know O speech how the buds beneath you are
    folded?
Waiting in gloom, protected by frost,
The dirt receding before my prophetical screams,
I underlying causes to balance them at last,
My knowledge my live parts, it keeping tally with the
    meaning of all things,
Happiness, (which whoever hears me let him or her set
    out in search of this day.)

My final merit I refuse you, I refuse putting from me what
    I really am,
Encompass worlds, but never try to encompass me,
I crowd your sleekest and best by simply looking toward
    you.

Writing and talk do not prove me,
I carry the plenum of proof and every thing else in my
    face,
With the hush of my lips I wholly confound the skeptic.

26

Now I will do nothing but listen,
To accrue what I hear into this song, to let sounds
     contribute toward it.

I hear bravuras of birds, bustle of growing wheat, gossip
     of flames, clack of sticks cooking my meals,
I hear the sound I love, the sound of the human voice,
I hear all sounds running together, combined, fused or
     following,
Sounds of the city and sounds out of the city, sounds of the
     day and night,
Talkative young ones to those that like them, the loud
     laugh of work-people at their meals,
The angry base of disjointed friendship, the faint tones of
     the sick,
The judge with hands tight to the desk, his pallid lips
     pronouncing a death-sentence,
The heave'e'yo of stevedores unlading ships by the
     wharves, the refrain of the anchor-lifters,
The ring of alarm-bells, the cry of fire, the whirr of
     swift-streaking engines and hose-carts with premonitory
     tinkles and color'd lights,
The steam-whistle, the solid roll of the train of approaching
     cars,
The slow march play'd at the head of the association
     marching two and two,
(They go to guard some corpse, the flag-tops are draped
     with black muslin.)

I hear the violoncello, ('tis the young man's heart's
     complaint,)
I hear the key'd cornet, it glides quickly in through my ears,
It shakes mad-sweet pangs through my belly and breast.

I hear the chorus, it is a grand opera,
Ah this indeed is music – this suits me.

A tenor large and fresh as the creation fills me,
The orbic flex of his mouth is pouring and filling me full.

I hear the train'd soprano (what work with hers is this?)
The orchestra whirls me wider than Uranus flies,
It wrenches such ardors from me I did not know I
    possess'd them,
It sails me, I dab with bare feet, they are lick'd by the
    indolent waves,
I am cut by bitter and angry hail, I lose my breath,
Steep'd amid honey'd morphine, my windpipe throttled in
    fakes of death,
At length let up again to feel the puzzle of puzzles,
And that we call Being.

27

To be in any form, what is that?
(Round and round we go, all of us, and ever come back
    thither,)
If nothing lay more develop'd the quahaug in its callous
    shell were enough.

Mine is no callous shell,
I have instant conductors all over me whether I pass or
    stop,
They seize every object and lead it harmlessly through me.

I merely stir, press, feel with my fingers, and am happy,
To touch my person to some one else's is about as much
    as I can stand.

28

Is this then a touch? quivering me to a new identity,
Flames and ether making a rush for my veins,
Treacherous tip of me reaching and crowding to help
 them,
My flesh and blood playing out lightning to strike what is
 hardly different from myself,
On all sides prurient provokers stiffening my limbs,
Straining the udder of my heart for its withheld drip,
Behaving licentious toward me, taking no denial,
Depriving me of my best as for a purpose,
Unbuttoning my clothes, holding me by the bare waist,
Deluding my confusion with the calm of the sunlight and
 pasture-fields,
Immodestly sliding the fellow-senses away,
They bribed to swap off with touch and go and graze at
 the edges of me,
No consideration, no regard for my draining strength or
 my anger,
Fetching the rest of the herd around to enjoy them a while,
Then all uniting to stand on a headland and worry me.

The sentries desert every other part of me,
They have left me helpless to a red marauder,
They all come to the headland to witness and assist against
 me.

I am given up by traitors,
I talk wildly, I have lost my wits, I and nobody else am
 the greatest traitor,
I went myself first to the headland, my own hands carried
 me there.

You villain touch! what are you doing? my breath is tight
   in its throat,
Unclench your floodgates, you are too much for me.

29

Blind loving wrestling touch, sheath'd hooded sharp-tooth'd
   touch!
Did it make you ache so, leaving me?

Parting track'd by arriving, perpetual payment of perpetual
   loan,
Rich showering rain, and recompense richer afterward.

Sprouts take and accumulate, stand by the curb prolific
   and vital,
Landscapes projected masculine, full-sized and golden.

30

All truths wait in all things,
They neither hasten their own delivery nor resist it,
They do not need the obstetric forceps of the surgeon,
The insignificant is as big to me as any,
(What is less or more than a touch?)

Logic and sermons never convince,
The damp of the night drives deeper into my soul.

(Only what proves itself to every man and woman is so,
Only what nobody denies is so.)

A minute and a drop of me settle my brain,
I believe the soggy clods shall become lovers and lamps,
And a compend of compends is the meat of a man or
   woman,

And a summit and flower there is the feeling they have for
    each other,
And they are to branch boundlessly out of that lesson until
    it becomes omnific,
And until one and all shall delight us, and we them.

31

I believe a leaf of grass is no less than the journey-work
    of the stars,
And the pismire is equally perfect, and a grain of sand,
    and the egg of the wren,
And the tree-toad is a chef-d'œuvre for the highest,
And the running blackberry would adorn the parlors of
    heaven,
And the narrowest hinge in my hand puts to scorn all
    machinery,
And the cow crunching with depress'd head surpasses any
    statue,
And a mouse is miracle enough to stagger sextillions of
    infidels.

I find I incorporate gneiss, coal, long-threaded moss, fruits,
    grains, esculent roots,
And am stucco'd with quadrupeds and birds all over,
And have distanced what is behind me for good reasons,
But call any thing back again when I desire it.

In vain the speeding or shyness,
In vain the plutonic rocks send their old heat against my
    approach,
In vain the mastodon retreats beneath its own powder'd
    bones,
In vain objects stand leagues off and assume manifold
    shapes,

In vain the ocean settling in hollows and the great
  monsters lying low,
In vain the buzzard houses herself with the sky,
In vain the snake slides through the creepers and logs,
In vain the elk takes to the inner passes of the woods,
In vain the razor-bill'd auk sails far north to Labrador,
I follow quickly, I ascend to the nest in the fissure of the
  cliff.

32

I think I could turn and live with animals, they are so
  placid and self-contain'd,
I stand and look at them long and long.

They do not sweat and whine about their condition,
They do not lie awake in the dark and weep for their sins,
They do not make me sick discussing their duty to God,
Not one is dissatisfied, not one is demented with the mania
  of owning things,
Not one kneels to another, nor to his kind that lived
  thousands of years ago,
Not one is respectable or unhappy over the whole earth.

So they show their relations to me and I accept them,
They bring me tokens of myself, they evince them plainly
  in their possession.

I wonder where they get those tokens,
Did I pass that way huge times ago and negligently drop
  them?

Myself moving forward then and now and forever,
Gathering and showing more always and with velocity,
Infinite and omnigenous, and the like of these among them,

Not too exclusive toward the reachers of my
    remembrancers,
Picking out here one that I love, and now go with him on
    brotherly terms.

A gigantic beauty of a stallion, fresh and responsive to my
    caresses,
Head high in the forehead, wide between the ears,
Limbs glossy and supple, tail dusting the ground,
Eyes full of sparkling wickedness, ears finely cut, flexibly
    moving.

His nostrils dilate as my heels embrace him,
His well-built limbs tremble with pleasure as we race
    around and return.

I but use you a minute, then I resign you, stallion,
Why do I need your paces when I myself out-gallop them?
Even as I stand or sit passing faster than you.

33

Space and Time! now I see it is true, what I guess'd at,
What I guess'd when I loaf'd on the grass,
What I guess'd while I lay alone in my bed,
And again as I walk'd the beach under the paling stars of
    the morning.

My ties and ballasts leave me, my elbows rest in sea-gaps,
I skirt sierras, my palms cover continents,
I am afoot with my vision.

By the city's quadrangular houses – in log huts, camping
    with lumbermen,
Along the ruts of the turnpike, along the dry gulch and
    rivulet bed,

Weeding my onion-patch or hoeing rows of carrots and
    parsnips, crossing savannas, trailing in forests,
Prospecting, gold-digging, girdling the trees of a new
    purchase,
Scorch'd ankle-deep by the hot sand, hauling by boat
    down the shallow river,
Where the panther walks to and fro on a limb overhead,
    where the buck turns furiously at the hunter,
Where the rattlesnake suns his flabby length on a rock,
    where the otter is feeding on fish,
Where the alligator in his tough pimples sleeps by the
    bayou,
Where the black bear is searching for roots or honey,
    where the beaver pats the mud with his paddle-shaped tail;
Over the growing sugar, over the yellow-flower'd cotton
    plant, over the rice in its low moist field,
Over the sharp-peak'd farm house, with its scallop'd
    scum and slender shoots from the gutters,
Over the western persimmon, over the long-leav'd corn,
    over the delicate blue-flower flax,
Over the white and brown buckwheat, a hummer and
    buzzer there with the rest,
Over the dusky green of the rye as it ripples and shades
    in the breeze;
Scaling mountains, pulling myself cautiously up, holding
    on by low scragged limbs,
Walking the path worn in the grass and beat through the
    leaves of the brush,
Where the quail is whistling betwixt the woods and the
    wheat-lot,
Where the bat flies in the Seventh-month eve, where the
    great goldbug drops through the dark,
Where the brook puts out of the roots of the old tree and
    flows to the meadow,

Where cattle stand and shake away flies with the tremulous
    shuddering of their hides.

Where the cheese-cloth hangs in the kitchen, where
    andirons straddle the hearth-slab, where cobwebs fall
    in festoons from the rafters;

Where trip-hammers crash, where the press is whirling
    its cylinders,

Wherever the human heart beats with terrible throes
    under its ribs,

Where the pear-shaped balloon is floating aloft, (floating
    in it myself and looking composedly down,)

Where the life-car is drawn on the slip-noose, where the
    heat hatches pale-green eggs in the dented sand,

Where the she-whale swims with her calf and never
    forsakes it,

Where the steam-ship trails hind-ways its long pennant of
    smoke,

Where the fin of the shark cuts like a black chip out of the
    water,

Where the half-burn'd brig is riding on unknown currents,

Where shells grow to her slimy deck, where the dead are
    corrupting below;

Where the dense-starr'd flag is borne at the head of the
    regiments,

Approaching Manhattan up by the long-stretching island,

Under Niagara, the cataract falling like a veil over my
    countenance,

Upon a door-step, upon the horse-block of hard wood
    outside,

Upon the race-course, or enjoying picnics or jigs or a good
    game of baseball,

At he-festivals, with blackguard gibes, ironical license,
    bull-dances, drinking, laughter,

At the cider-mill tasting the sweets of the brown mash,
  sucking the juice through a straw,
At apple-peelings wanting kisses for all the red fruit I find,
At musters, beach-parties, friendly bees, huskings,
  house-raisings;
Where the mocking-bird sounds his delicious gurgles,
  cackles, screams, weeps,
Where the hay-rick stands in the barn-yard, where the
  dry-stalks are scatter'd, where the brood-cow waits in
  the hovel,
Where the bull advances to do his masculine work, where
  the stud to the mare, where the cock is treading the hen,
Where the heifers browse, where geese nip their food with
  short jerks,
Where sun-down shadows lengthen over the limitless and
  lonesome prairie,
Where herds of buffalo make a crawling spread of the
  square miles far and near,
Where the humming-bird shimmers, where the neck of the
  long-lived swan is curving and winding,
Where the laughing-gull scoots by the shore, where she
  laughs her near-human laugh,
Where bee-hives range on a gray bench in the garden half
  hid by the high weeds,
Where band-neck'd partridges roost in a ring on the
  ground with their heads out,
Where burial coaches enter the arch'd gates of a cemetery,
Where winter wolves bark amid wastes of snow and icicled
  trees,
Where the yellow-crown'd heron comes to the edge of the
  marsh at night and feeds upon small crabs,
Where the splash of swimmers and divers cools the warm
  noon,

Where the katy-did works her chromatic reed on the
    walnut-tree over the well,
Through patches of citrons and cucumbers with
    silver-wired leaves,
Through the salt-lick or orange glade, or under conical
    firs,
Through the gymnasium, through the curtain'd saloon,
    through the office or public hall;
Pleas'd with the native and pleas'd with the foreign, pleas'd
    with the new and old,
Pleas'd with the homely woman as well as the handsome,
Pleas'd with the quakeress as she puts off her bonnet and
    talks melodiously,
Pleas'd with the tune of the choir of the whitewash'd
    church,
Pleas'd with the earnest words of the sweating Methodist
    preacher, impress'd seriously at the camp-meeting;
Looking in at the shop windows of Broadway the whole
    forenoon, flatting the flesh of my nose on the thick plate
    glass,
Wandering the same afternoon with my face turn'd up to
    the clouds, or down a lane or along the beach,
My right and left arms round the sides of two friends, and
    I in the middle;
Coming home with the silent and dark-cheek'd bush-boy,
    (behind me he rides at the drape of the day,)
Far from the settlements studying the print of animals'
    feet, or the moccasin print,
By the cot in the hospital reaching lemonade to a feverish
    patient,
Nigh the coffin'd corpse when all is still, examining with a
    candle;
Voyaging to every port to dicker and adventure,
Hurrying with the modern crowd as eager and fickle as any,

Hot toward one I hate, ready in my madness to knife him,
Solitary at midnight in my back yard, my thoughts gone
    from me a long while,
Walking the old hills of Judæa with the beautiful gentle
    God by my side,
Speeding through space, speeding through heaven and the
    stars,
Speeding amid the seven satellites and the broad ring, and
    the diameter of eighty thousand miles,
Speeding with tail'd meteors, throwing fire-balls like the
    rest,
Carrying the crescent child that carries its own full mother
    in its belly,
Storming, enjoying, planning, loving, cautioning,
My voice is the wife's voice, the screech by the rail of the
    stairs,
They fetch my man's body up dripping and drown'd.

I understand the large hearts of heroes,
The courage of present times and all times,
How the skipper saw the crowded and rudderless wreck
    of the steam-ship, and Death chasing it up and down
    the storm,
How he knuckled tight and gave not back an inch, and
    was faithful of days and faithful of nights,
And chalk'd in large letters on a board, *Be of good cheer,
    we will not desert you;*
How he follow'd with them and tack'd with them three
    days and would not give it up,
How he saved the drifting company at last,
How the lank loose-gown'd women look'd when boated
    from the side of their prepared graves,
How the silent old-faced infants and the lifted sick, and
    the sharp-lipp'd unshaved men;

All this I swallow, it tastes good, I like it well, it becomes
   mine,
I am the man, I suffer'd, I was there.

The disdain and calmness of martyrs,
The mother of old, condemn'd for a witch, burnt with dry
   wood, her children gazing on,
The hounded slave that flags in the race, leans by the
   fence, blowing, cover'd with sweat,
The twinges that sting like needles his legs and neck, the
   murderous buckshot and the bullets,
All these I feel or am.

I am the hounded slave, I wince at the bite of the dogs,
Hell and despair are upon me, crack and again crack the
   marksmen,
I clutch the rails of the fence, my gore dribs, thinn'd
   with the ooze of my skin,
I fall on the weeds and stones,
The riders spur their unwilling horses, haul close,
Taunt my dizzy ears and beat me violently over the head
   with whip-stocks.

Agonies are one of my changes of garments,
I do not ask the wounded person how he feels, I myself
   become the wounded person,
My hurts turn livid upon me as I lean on a cane and
   observe.

I am the mash'd fireman with breast-bone broken,
Tumbling walls buried me in their debris,
Heat and smoke I inspired, I heard the yelling shouts of
   my comrades,
I heard the distant click of their picks and shovels,
They have clear'd the beams away, they tenderly lift me
   forth.

I lie in the night air in my red shirt, the pervading hush
   is for my sake,
Painless after all I lie exhausted but not so unhappy,
White and beautiful are the faces around me, the heads
   are bared of their fire-caps,
The kneeling crowd fades with the light of the torches.

Distant and dead resuscitate,
They show as the dial or move as the hands of me, I am
   the clock myself.

I am an old artillerist, I tell of my fort's bombardment,
I am there again.

Again the long roll of the drummers,
Again the attacking cannon, mortars,
Again to my listening ears the cannon responsive.

I take part, I see and hear the whole,
The cries, curses, roar, the plaudits for well-aim'd shots,
The ambulanza slowly passing trailing its red drip,
Workmen searching after damages, making indispensable
   repairs,
The fall of grenades through the rent roof, the fan-shaped
   explosion,
The whizz of limbs, heads, stone, wood, iron, high in the
   air.

Again gurgles the mouth of my dying general, he furiously
   waves with his hand,
He gasps through the clot *Mind not me – mind – the
entrenchments.*

34

Now I tell what I knew in Texas in my early youth,
(I tell not the fall of Alamo,
Not one escaped to tell the fall of Alamo,
The hundred and fifty are dumb yet at Alamo,)
'Tis the tale of the murder in cold blood of four hundred
    and twelve young men.

Retreating they had form'd in a hollow square with their
    baggage for breastworks,
Nine hundred lives out of the surrounding enemy's, nine
    times their number, was the price they took in advance,
Their colonel was wounded and their ammunition gone,
They treated for an honorable capitulation, receiv'd writing
    and seal, gave up their arms and march'd back prisoners
    of war.

They were the glory of the race of rangers,
Matchless with horse, rifle, song, supper, courtship,
Large, turbulent, generous, handsome, proud, and
    affectionate,
Bearded, sunburnt, drest in the free costume of hunters,
Not a single one over thirty years of age.

The second First-day morning they were brought out in
    squads and massacred, it was beautiful early summer,
The work commenced about five o'clock and was over
    by eight.

None obey'd the command to kneel,
Some made a mad and helpless rush, some stood stark and
    straight,
A few fell at once, shot in the temple or heart, the living
    and dead lay together,

The maim'd and mangled dug in the dirt, the new-comers
saw them there,
Some half-kill'd attempted to crawl away,
These were despatch'd with bayonets or batter'd with the
blunts of muskets,
A youth not seventeen years old seiz'd his assassin till
two more came to release him,
The three were all torn and cover'd with the boy's blood.

At eleven o'clock began the burning of the bodies;
That is the tale of the murder of the four hundred and
twelve young men.

35

Would you hear of an old-time sea-fight?
Would you learn who won by the light of the moon and
stars?
List to the yarn, as my grandmother's father the sailor
told it to me.

Our foe was no skulk in his ship I tell you, (said he,)
His was the surly English pluck, and there is no tougher
or truer, and never was, and never will be;
Along the lower'd eve he came horribly raking us.

We closed with him, the yards entangled, the cannon
touch'd,
My captain lash'd fast with his own hands.

We had receiv'd some eighteen pound shots under the
water,
On our lower-gun-deck two large pieces had burst at the
first fire, killing all around and blowing up overhead.

Fighting at sun-down, fighting at dark,
Ten o'clock at night, the full moon well up, our leaks on
the gain, and five feet of water reported,
The master-at-arms loosing the prisoners confined in the
after-hold to give them a chance for themselves.

The transit to and from the magazine is now stopt by the
sentinels,
They see so many strange faces they do not know whom to
trust.

Our frigate takes fire,
The other asks if we demand quarter?
If our colors are struck and the fighting done?

Now I laugh content, for I hear the voice of my little
captain,
We have not struck, he composedly cries, *we have just
begun our part of the fighting.*

Only three guns are in use,
One is directed by the captain himself against the enemy's
mainmast,
Two well serv'd with grape and canister silence his
musketry and clear his decks.

The tops alone second the fire of this little battery,
especially the main-top,
They hold out bravely during the whole of the action.

Not a moment's cease,
The leaks gain fast on the pumps, the fire eats toward
the powder-magazine.

One of the pumps has been shot away, it is generally
   thought we are sinking.

Serene stands the little captain,
He is not hurried, his voice is neither high nor low,
His eyes give more light to us than our battle-lanterns.

Toward twelve there in the beams of the moon they
   surrender to us.

36

Stretch'd and still lies the midnight,
Two great hulls motionless on the breast of the darkness,
Our vessel riddled and slowly sinking, preparations to
   pass to the one we have conquer'd,
The captain on the quarter-deck coldly giving his orders
   through a countenance white as a sheet,
Near by the corpse of the child that serv'd in the cabin,
The dead face of an old salt with long white hair and
   carefully curl'd whiskers,
The flames spite of all that can be done flickering aloft
   and below,
The husky voices of the two or three officers yet fit for
   duty,
Formless stacks of bodies and bodies by themselves,
   dabs of flesh upon the masts and spars,
Cut of cordage, dangle of rigging, slight shock of the
   soothe of waves,
Black and impassive guns, litter of powder-parcels, strong
   scent,
A few large stars overhead, silent and mournful shining,
Delicate sniffs of sea-breeze, smells of sedgy grass and
   fields by the shore, death-messages given in charge to
   survivors,

The hiss of the surgeon's knife, the gnawing teeth of his
    saw,
Wheeze, cluck, swash of falling blood, short wild scream,
    and long, dull, tapering groan,
These so, these irretrievable.

37

You laggards there on guard! look to your arms!
In at the conquer'd doors they crowd! I am possess'd!
Embody all presences outlaw'd or suffering,
See myself in prison shaped like another man,
And feel the dull unintermitted pain.

For me the keepers of convicts shoulder their carbines
    and keep watch,
It is I let out in the morning and barr'd at night.

Not a mutineer walks handcuff'd to jail but I am handcuff'd
    to him and walk by his side,
(I am less the jolly one there, and more the silent one with
    sweat on my twitching lips.)

Not a youngster is taken for larceny but I go up too, and
    am tried and sentenced.

Not a cholera patient lies at the last gasp but I also lie
    at the last gasp,
My face is ash-color'd, my sinews gnarl, away from me
    people retreat.

Askers embody themselves in me and I am embodied in
    them,
I project my hat, sit shame-faced, and beg.

38

Enough! enough! enough!
Somehow I have been stunn'd. Stand back!
Give me a little time beyond my cuff'd head, slumbers,
    dreams, gaping,
I discover myself on the verge of a usual mistake.

That I could forget the mockers and insults!
That I could forget the trickling tears and the blows of the
    bludgeons and hammers!
That I could look with a separate look on my own
    crucifixion and bloody crowning.

I remember now,
I resume the overstaid fraction,
The grave of rock multiplies what has been confided to
    it, or to any graves,
Corpses rise, gashes heal, fastenings roll from me.

I troop forth replenish'd with supreme power, one of an
    average unending procession,
Inland and sea-coast we go, and pass all boundary lines,
Our swift ordinances on their way over the whole earth,
The blossoms we wear in our hats the growth of thousands
    of years.

Eleves, I salute you! come forward!
Continue your annotations, continue your questionings.

39

The friendly and flowing savage, who is he?
Is he waiting for civilization, or past it and mastering it?

Is he some Southwesterner rais'd out-doors? is he
    Kanadian?
Is he from the Mississippi country? Iowa, Oregon,
    California?
The mountains? prairie-life, bush-life? or sailor from the
    sea?

Wherever he goes men and women accept and desire him,
They desire he should like them, touch them, speak to
    them, stay with them.

Behavior lawless as snow-flakes, words simple as grass,
    uncomb'd head, laughter, and naivetè,
Slow-stepping feet, common features, common modes and
    emanations,
They descend in new forms from the tips of his fingers,
They are wafted with the odor of his body or breath, they
    fly out of the glance of his eyes.

40

Flaunt of the sunshine I need not your bask – lie over!
You light surfaces only, I force surfaces and depths also.

Earth! you seem to look for something at my hands,
Say, old top-knot, what do you want?

Man or woman, I might tell how I like you, but cannot,
And might tell what it is in me and what it is in you, but
    cannot,
And might tell what pining I have, that pulse of my
    nights and days.

Behold, I do not give lectures or a little charity,
When I give I give myself.

You there, impotent, loose in the knees,
Open your scarf'd chops till I blow grit within you,
Spread your palms and lift the flaps of your pockets,
I am not to be denied, I compel, I have stores plenty and
    to spare,
And any thing I have I bestow.

I do not ask who you are, that is not important to me,
You can do nothing and be nothing but what I will infold
    you.

To cotton-field drudge or cleaner of privies I lean,
On his right cheek I put the family kiss,
And in my soul I swear I never will deny him.

On women fit for conception I start bigger and nimbler
    babes,
(This day I am jetting the stuff of far more arrogant
    republics.)

To any one dying, thither I speed and twist the knob of
    the door,
Turn the bed-clothes toward the foot of the bed,
Let the physician and the priest go home.

I seize the descending man and raise him with resistless
    will,
O despairer, here is my neck,
By God, you shall not go down! hang your whole weight
    upon me.

I dilate you with tremendous breath, I buoy you up,
Every room of the house do I fill with an arm'd force,
Lovers of me, bafflers of graves.

Sleep – I and they keep guard all night,
Not doubt, not decease shall dare to lay finger upon you,
I have embraced you, and henceforth possess you to myself,
And when you rise in the morning you will find what I
    tell you is so.

41

I am he bringing help for the sick as they pant on their
    backs,
And for strong upright men I bring yet more needed
    help.

I heard what was said of the universe,
Heard it and heard it of several thousand years;
It is middling well as far as it goes – but is that all?

Magnifying and applying come I,
Outbidding at the start the old cautious hucksters,
Taking myself the exact dimensions of Jehovah,
Lithographing Kronos, Zeus his son, and Hercules his
    grandson,
Buying drafts of Osiris, Isis, Belus, Brahma, Buddha,
In my portfolio placing Manito loose, Allah on a leaf, the
    crucifix engraved,
With Odin and the hideous-faced Mexitli and every idol
    and image,
Taking them all for what they are worth and not a cent
    more,
Admitting they were alive and did the work of their days,
(They bore mites as for unfledg'd birds who have now to
    rise and fly and sing for themselves,)
Accepting the rough deific sketches to fill out better in
    myself, bestowing them freely on each man and woman
    I see,

Discovering as much or more in a framer framing a house,
Putting higher claims for him there with his roll'd-up
    sleeves driving the mallet and chisel,
Not objecting to special revelations, considering a curl of
    smoke or a hair on the back of my hand just as curious
    as any revelation,
Lads ahold of fire-engines and hook-and-ladder ropes no
    less to me than the gods of the antique wars,
Minding their voices peal through the crash of destruction,
Their brawny limbs passing safe over charr'd laths, their
    white foreheads whole and unhurt out of the flames;
By the mechanic's wife with her babe at her nipple
    interceding for every person born,
Three scythes at harvest whizzing in a row from three
    lusty angels with shirts bagg'd out at their waists,
The snag-tooth'd hostler with red hair redeeming sins
    past and to come,
Selling all he possesses, traveling on foot to fee lawyers
    for his brother and sit by him while he is tried for
    forgery;
What was strewn in the amplest strewing the square rod
    about me, and not filling the square rod then,
The bull and the bug never worshipp'd half enough,
Dung and dirt more admirable than was dream'd,
The supernatural of no account, myself waiting my time
    to be one of the supremes,
The day getting ready for me when I shall do as much
    good as the best, and be as prodigious;
By my life-lumps! becoming already a creator,
Putting myself here and now to the ambush'd womb of
    the shadows.

42

A call in the midst of the crowd,
My own voice, orotund sweeping and final.

Come my children,
Come my boys and girls, my women, household and
    intimates,
Now the performer launches his nerve, he has pass'd his
    prelude on the reeds within.

Easily written loose-finger'd chords – I feel the thrum
    of your climax and close.

My head slues round on my neck,
Music rolls, but not from the organ,
Folks are around me, but they are no household of mine.

Ever the hard unsunk ground,
Ever the eaters and drinkers, ever the upward and
    downward sun, ever the air and the ceaseless tides,
Ever myself and my neighbors, refreshing, wicked, real,
Ever the old inexplicable query, ever that thorn'd thumb,
    that breath of itches and thirsts,
Ever the vexer's *hoot! hoot!* till we find where the sly one
    hides and bring him forth,
Ever love, ever the sobbing liquid of life,
Ever the bandage under the chin, ever the trestles of death.

Here and there with dimes on the eyes walking,
To feed the greed of the belly the brains liberally spooning,
Tickets buying, taking, selling, but in to the feast never
    once going,

Many sweating, ploughing, thrashing, and then the chaff
  for payment receiving,
A few idly owning, and they the wheat continually
  claiming.

This is the city and I am one of the citizens,
Whatever interests the rest interests me, politics, wars,
  markets, newspapers, schools,
The mayor and councils, banks, tariffs, steamships,
  factories, stocks, stores, real estate and personal estate.

The little plentiful manikins skipping around in collars
  and tail'd coats,
I am aware who they are, (they are positively not worms or
  fleas,)
I acknowledge the duplicates of myself, the weakest and
  shallowest is deathless with me,
What I do and say the same waits for them,
Every thought that flounders in me the same flounders in
  them.

I know perfectly well my own egotism,
Know my omnivorous lines and must not write any less,
And would fetch you whoever you are flush with myself.

Not words of routine this song of mine,
But abruptly to question, to leap beyond yet nearer bring;
This printed and bound book – but the printer and the
  printing-office boy?

The well-taken photographs – but your wife or friend
  close and solid in your arms?
The black ship mail'd with iron, her mighty guns in her
  turrets – but the pluck of the captain and engineers?

In the houses the dishes and fare and furniture – but the
    host and hostess, and the look out of their eyes?
The sky up there – yet here or next door, or across the way?
The saints and sages in history – but you yourself?
Sermons, creeds, theology – but the fathomless human
    brain,
And what is reason? and what is love? and what is life?

43

I do not despise you priests, all time, the world over,
My faith is the greatest of faiths and the least of faiths,
Enclosing worship ancient and modern and all between
    ancient and modern,
Believing I shall come again upon the earth after five
    thousand years,
Waiting responses from oracles, honoring the gods, saluting
    the sun,
Making a fetich of the first rock or stump, powowing with
    sticks in the circle of obis,
Helping the llama or brahmin as he trims the lamps of the
    idols,
Dancing yet through the streets in a phallic procession,
    rapt and austere in the woods a gymnosophist,
Drinking mead from the skull-cap, to Shastas and Vedas
    admirant, minding the Koran,
Walking the teokallis, spotted with gore from the stone
    and knife, beating the serpent-skin drum,
Accepting the Gospels, accepting him that was crucified,
    knowing assuredly that he is divine,
To the mass kneeling or the puritan's prayer rising, or
    sitting patiently in a pew,
Ranting and frothing in my insane crisis, or waiting
    dead-like till my spirit arouses me,

Looking forth on pavement and land, or outside of
  pavement and land,
Belonging to the winders of the circuit of circuits.

One of that centripetal and centrifugal gang I turn and
  talk like a man leaving charges before a journey.

Down-hearted doubters dull and excluded,
Frivolous, sullen, moping, angry, affected, dishearten'd,
  atheistical,
I know every one of you, I know the sea of torment,
  doubt, despair and unbelief.

How the flukes splash!
How they contort rapid as lightning, with spasms and
  spouts of blood!

Be at peace bloody flukes of doubters and sullen mopers,
I take my place among you as much as among any,
The past is the push of you, me, all precisely the same,
And what is yet untried and afterward is for you, me, all,
  precisely the same.

I do not know what is untried and afterward,
But I know it will in its turn prove sufficient, and cannot
  fail.

Each who passes is consider'd, each who stops is consider'd,
  not a single one can it fail.

It cannot fail the young man who died and was buried,
Nor the young woman who died and was put by his side,
Nor the little child that peep'd in at the door, and then
  drew back and was never seen again,

Nor the old man who has lived without purpose, and feels
  it with bitterness worse than gall,
Nor him in the poor house tubercled by rum and the bad
  disorder,
Nor the numberless slaughter'd and wreck'd, nor the
  brutish koboo call'd the ordure of humanity,
Nor the sacs merely floating with open mouths for food to
  slip in,
Nor any thing in the earth, or down in the oldest graves
  of the earth,
Nor any thing in the myriads of spheres, nor the myriads
  of myriads that inhabit them,
Nor the present, nor the least wisp that is known.

44

It is time to explain myself – let us stand up.

What is known I strip away,
I launch all men and women forward with me into the
  Unknown.

The clock indicates the moment – but what does eternity
  indicate?

We have thus far exhausted trillions of winters and
  summers,
There are trillions ahead, and trillions ahead of them.

Births have brought us richness and variety,
And other births will bring us richness and variety.

I do not call one greater and one smaller,
That which fills its period and place is equal to any.

Were mankind murderous or jealous upon you, my
    brother, my sister?
I am sorry for you, they are not murderous or jealous
    upon me,
All has been gentle with me, I keep no account with
    lamentation,
(What have I to do with lamentation?)

I am an acme of things accomplish'd, and I am encloser
    of things to be.

My feet strike an apex of the apices of the stairs,
On every step bunches of ages, and larger bunches between
    the steps,
All below duly travel'd, and still I mount and mount.

Rise after rise bow the phantoms behind me,
Afar down I see the huge first Nothing, I know I was
    even there,
I waited unseen and always, and slept through the lethargic
    mist,
And took my time, and took no hurt from the fetid carbon.

Long I was hugg'd close – long and long.

Immense have been the preparations for me,
Faithful and friendly the arms that have help'd me.

Cycles ferried my cradle, rowing and rowing like cheerful
    boatmen,
For room to me stars kept aside in their own rings,
They sent influences to look after what was to hold me.

Before I was born out of my mother generations guided me,
My embryo has never been torpid, nothing could overlay it.

For it the nebula cohered to an orb,
The long slow strata piled to rest it on,
Vast vegetables gave it sustenance,
Monstrous sauroids transported it in their mouths and
  deposited it with care.

All forces have been steadily employ'd to complete and
  delight me,
Now on this spot I stand with my robust soul.

45

O span of youth! ever-push'd elasticity!
O manhood, balanced, florid and full.

My lovers suffocate me,
Crowding my lips, thick in the pores of my skin,
Jostling me through streets and public halls, coming naked
  to me at night,
Crying by day *Ahoy!* from the rocks of the river, swinging
  and chirping over my head,
Calling my name from flower-beds, vines, tangled
  underbrush,
Lighting on every moment of my life,
Bussing my body with soft balsamic busses,
Noiselessly passing handfuls out of their hearts and giving
  them to be mine.

Old age superbly rising! O welcome, ineffable grace of
  dying days!

Every condition promulges not only itself, it promulges
  what grows after and out of itself,
And the dark hush promulges as much as any.

I open my scuttle at night and see the far-sprinkled
   systems,
And all I see multiplied as high as I can cipher edge but
   the rim of the farther systems.

Wider and wider they spread, expanding, always expanding,
Outward and outward and forever outward.

My sun has his sun and round him obediently wheels,
He joins with his partners a group of superior circuit,
And greater sets follow, making specks of the greatest
   inside them.

There is no stoppage and never can be stoppage,
If I, you, and the worlds, and all beneath or upon their
   surfaces, were this moment reduced back to a pallid
   float, it would not avail in the long run,
We should surely bring up again where we now stand,
And surely go as much farther, and then farther and
   farther.

A few quadrillions of eras, a few octillions of cubic
   leagues, do not hazard the span or make it impatient,
They are but parts, any thing is but a part.

See ever so far, there is limitless space outside of that,
Count ever so much, there is limitless time around that.

My rendezvous is appointed, it is certain,
The Lord will be there and wait till I come on perfect
   terms,
The great Camerado, the lover true for whom I pine will
   be there.

46

I know I have the best of time and space, and was never
    measured and never will be measured.

I tramp a perpetual journey, (come listen all!)
My signs are a rain-proof coat, good shoes, and a staff cut
    from the woods,
No friend of mine takes his ease in my chair,
I have no chair, no church, no philosophy,
I lead no man to a dinner-table, library, exchange,
But each man and each woman of you I lead upon a knoll,
My left hand hooking you round the waist,
My right hand pointing to landscapes of continents and
    the public road.

Not I, not any one else can travel that road for you,
You must travel it for yourself.

It is not far, it is within reach,
Perhaps you have been on it since you were born and did
    not know,
Perhaps it is everywhere on water and on land.

Shoulder your duds dear son, and I will mine, and let us
    hasten forth,
Wonderful cities and free nations we shall fetch as we go.

If you tire, give me both burdens, and rest the chuff of
    your hand on my hip,
And in due time you shall repay the same service to me,
For after we start we never lie by again.

This day before dawn I ascended a hill and look'd at the
crowded heaven,
And I said to my spirit *When we become the enfolders of
those orbs, and the pleasure and knowledge of every thing
in them, shall we be fill'd and satisfied then?*
And my spirit said *No, we but level that lift to pass and
continue beyond.*

You are also asking me questions and I hear you,
I answer that I cannot answer, you must find out for
yourself.

Sit a while dear son,
Here are biscuits to eat and here is milk to drink,
But as soon as you sleep and renew yourself in sweet
clothes, I kiss you with a good-by kiss and open the
gate for your egress hence.

Long enough have you dream'd contemptible dreams,
Now I wash the gum from your eyes,
You must habit yourself to the dazzle of the light and of
every moment of your life.

Long have you timidly waded holding a plank by the shore,
Now I will you to be a bold swimmer,
To jump off in the midst of the sea, rise again, nod to me,
shout, and laughingly dash with your hair.

47

I am the teacher of athletes,
He that by me spreads a wider breast than my own proves
the width of my own,
He most honors my style who learns under it to destroy
the teacher.

The boy I love, the same becomes a man not through
    derived power, but in his own right,
Wicked rather than virtuous out of conformity or fear,
Fond of his sweetheart, relishing well his steak,
Unrequited love or a slight cutting him worse than sharp
    steel cuts,
First-rate to ride, to fight, to hit the bull's eye, to sail a
    skiff, to sing a song or play on the banjo,
Preferring scars and the beard and faces pitted with
    small-pox over all latherers,
And those well-tann'd to those that keep out of the sun.

I teach straying from me, yet who can stray from me?
I follow you whoever you are from the present hour,
My words itch at your ears till you understand them.

I do not say these things for a dollar or to fill up the time
    while I wait for a boat,
(It is you talking just as much as myself, I act as the
    tongue of you,
Tied in your mouth, in mine it begins to be loosen'd.)

I swear I will never again mention love or death inside
    a house,
And I swear I will never translate myself at all, only to
    him or her who privately stays with me in the open air.

If you would understand me go to the heights or
    water-shore,
The nearest gnat is an explanation, and a drop or motion
    of waves a key,
The maul, the oar, the hand-saw, second my words.

No shutter'd room or school can commune with me,
But roughs and little children better than they.

The young mechanic is closest to me, he knows me well,
The woodman that takes his axe and jug with him shall
    take me with him all day,
The farm-boy ploughing in the field feels good at the
    sound of my voice,
In vessels that sail my words sail, I go with fishermen and
    seamen and love them.

The soldier camp'd or upon the march is mine,
On the night ere the pending battle many seek me, and I
    do not fail them,
On that solemn night (it may be their last) those that know
    me seek me.

My face rubs to the hunter's face when he lies down alone
    in his blanket,
The driver thinking of me does not mind the jolt of his
    wagon,
The young mother and old mother comprehend me,
The girl and the wife rest the needle a moment and forget
    where they are,
They and all would resume what I have told them.

48

I have said that the soul is not more than the body,
And I have said that the body is not more than the soul,
And nothing, not God, is greater to one than one's self is,
And whoever walks a furlong without sympathy walks to
    his own funeral drest in his shroud,
And I or you pocketless of a dime may purchase the pick
    of the earth,
And to glance with an eye or show a bean in its pod
    confounds the learning of all times,

And there is no trade or employment but the young man
    following it may become a hero,
And there is no object so soft but it makes a hub for the
    wheel'd universe,
And I say to any man or woman, Let your soul stand cool
    and composed before a million universes.

And I say to mankind, Be not curious about God,
For I who am curious about each am not curious about
    God,
(No array of terms can say how much I am at peace about
    God and about death.)

I hear and behold God in every object, yet understand
    God not in the least,
Nor do I understand who there can be more wonderful
    than myself.

Why should I wish to see God better than this day?
I see something of God each hour of the twenty-four, and
    each moment then,
In the faces of men and women I see God, and in my own
    face in the glass,
I find letters from God dropt in the street, and every one
    is sign'd by God's name,
And I leave them where they are, for I know that
    wheresoe'er I go,
Others will punctually come for ever and ever.

49

And as to you Death, and you bitter hug of mortality, it is
    idle to try to alarm me.

To his work without flinching the accoucheur comes,
I see the elder-hand pressing receiving supporting,
I recline by the sills of the exquisite flexible doors,
And mark the outlet, and mark the relief and escape.

And as to you Corpse I think you are good manure, but
  that does not offend me,
I smell the white roses sweet-scented and growing,
I reach to the leafy lips, I reach to the polish'd breasts of
    melons.

And as to you Life I reckon you are the leavings of many
    deaths,
(No doubt I have died myself ten thousand times before.)

I hear you whispering there O stars of heaven,
O suns – O grass of graves – O perpetual transfers and
    promotions,
If you do not say any thing how can I say any thing?

Of the turbid pool that lies in the autumn forest,
Of the moon that descends the steeps of the soughing
    twilight,
Toss, sparkles of day and dusk – toss on the black stems
    that decay in the muck,
Toss to the moaning gibberish of the dry limbs.

I ascend from the moon, I ascend from the night,
I perceive that the ghastly glimmer is noonday sunbeams
    reflected,
And debouch to the steady and central from the offspring
    great or small.

50

There is that in me – I do not know what it is – but I
know it is in me.

Wrench'd and sweaty – calm and cool then my body
becomes,
I sleep – I sleep long.

I do not know it – it is without name – it is a word
unsaid,
It is not in any dictionary, utterance, symbol.

Something it swings on more than the earth I swing on,
To it the creation is the friend whose embracing awakes
me.

Perhaps I might tell more. Outlines! I plead for my
brothers and sisters.

Do you see O my brothers and sisters?
It is not chaos or death – it is form, union, plan – it is
eternal life – it is Happiness.

51

The past and present wilt – I have fill'd them, emptied
them,
And proceed to fill my next fold of the future.

Listener up there! what have you to confide to me?
Look in my face while I snuff the sidle of evening,
(Talk honestly, no one else hears you, and I stay only a
minute longer.)

Do I contradict myself?
Very well then I contradict myself,
(I am large, I contain multitudes.)

I concentrate toward them that are nigh, I wait on the
    door-slab.

Who has done his day's work? who will soonest be through
    with his supper?
Who wishes to walk with me?

Will you speak before I am gone? will you prove already
    too late?

52

The spotted hawk swoops by and accuses me, he complains
    of my gab and my loitering.

I too am not a bit tamed, I too am untranslatable,
I sound my barbaric yawp over the roofs of the world.

The last scud of day holds back for me,
It flings my likeness after the rest and true as any on the
    shadow'd wilds,
It coaxes me to the vapor and the dusk.

I depart as air, I shake my white locks at the runaway
    sun,
I effuse my flesh in eddies, and drift it in lacy jags.

I bequeath myself to the dirt to grow from the grass I love,
If you want me again look for me under your boot-soles.

You will hardly know who I am or what I mean,
But I shall be good health to you nevertheless,
And filter and fibre your blood.

Failing to fetch me at first keep encouraged,
Missing me one place search another,
I stop somewhere waiting for you.

1855

I Sing the Body Electric

I

I sing the body electric,
The armies of those I love engirth me and I engirth them,
They will not let me off till I go with them, respond to
    them,
And discorrupt them, and charge them full with the charge
    of the soul.

Was it doubted that those who corrupt their own bodies
    conceal themselves?
And if those who defile the living are as bad as they who
    defile the dead?
And if the body does not do fully as much as the soul?
And if the body were not the soul, what is the soul?

2

The love of the body of man or woman balks account,
    the body itself balks account,
That of the male is perfect, and that of the female is
    perfect.

The expression of the face balks account,
But the expression of a well-made man appears not only in
    his face,
It is in his limbs and joints also, it is curiously in the joints
    of his hips and wrists,
It is in his walk, the carriage of his neck, the flex of his
    waist and knees, dress does not hide him,
The strong sweet quality he has strikes through the cotton
    and broadcloth,

To see him pass conveys as much as the best poem,
    perhaps more,
You linger to see his back, and the back of his neck and
    shoulder-side.

The sprawl and fulness of babes, the bosoms and heads
    of women, the folds of their dress, their style as we pass
    in the street, the contour of their shape downwards,
The swimmer naked in the swimming-bath, seen as he
    swims through the transparent green-shine, or lies with
    his face up and rolls silently to and fro in the heave of
    the water,
The bending forward and backward of rowers in
    row-boats, the horseman in his saddle,
Girls, mothers, house-keepers, in all their performances,
The group of laborers seated at noon-time with their open
    dinner-kettles, and their wives waiting,
The female soothing a child, the farmer's daughter in the
    garden or cow-yard,
The young fellow hoeing corn, the sleigh-driver driving his
    six horses through the crowd,
The wrestle of wrestlers, two apprentice-boys, quite grown,
    lusty, good-natured, native-born, out on the vacant lot
    at sundown after work,
The coats and caps thrown down, the embrace of love and
    resistance,
The upper-hold and under-hold, the hair rumpled over
    and blinding the eyes;
The march of firemen in their own costumes, the play of
    masculine muscle through clean-setting trowsers and
    waist-straps,
The slow return from the fire, the pause when the bell
    strikes suddenly again, and the listening on the alert,

The natural, perfect, varied attitudes, the bent head, the
    curv'd neck and the counting;
Such-like I love – I loosen myself, pass freely, am at the
    mother's breast with the little child,
Swim with the swimmers, wrestle with wrestlers, march in
    line with the firemen, and pause, listen, count.

3

I knew a man, a common farmer, the father of five sons,
And in them the fathers of sons, and in them the fathers
    of sons.

This man was of wonderful vigor, calmness, beauty of
    person,
The shape of his head, the pale yellow and the white of
    his hair and beard, the immeasurable meaning of his
    black eyes, the richness and breadth of his manners,
These I used to go and visit him to see, he was wise also,
He was six feet tall, he was over eighty years old, his sons
    were massive, clean, bearded, tan-faced, handsome,
They and his daughters loved him, all who saw him loved
    him,
They did not love him by allowance, they loved him with
    personal love,
He drank water only, the blood show'd like scarlet through
    the clear-brown skin of his face,
He was a frequent gunner and fisher, he sail'd his boat
    himself, he had a fine one presented to him by a
    ship-joiner, he had fowling-pieces presented to him by
    men that loved him,
When he went with his five sons and many grand-sons
    to hunt or fish, you would pick him out as the most
    beautiful and vigorous of the gang,

You would wish long and long to be with him, you would
    wish to sit by him in the boat that you and he might
    touch each other.

4

I have perceiv'd that to be with those I like is enough,
To stop in company with the rest at evening is enough,
To be surrounded by beautiful, curious, breathing, laughing
    flesh is enough,
To pass among them or touch any one, or rest my arm
    ever so lightly round his or her neck for a moment, what
    is this then?
I do not ask any more delight, I swim in it as in a sea.

There is something in staying close to men and women
    and looking on them, and in the contact and odor of
    them, that pleases the soul well,
All things please the soul, but these please the soul well.

5

This is the female form,
A divine nimbus exhales from it from head to foot,
It attracts with fierce undeniable attraction,
I am drawn by its breath as if I were no more than a
    helpless vapor, all falls aside but myself and it,
Books, art, religion, time, the visible and solid earth,
    and what was expected of heaven or fear'd of hell, are
    now consumed,
Mad filaments, ungovernable shoots play out of it, the
    response likewise ungovernable,
Hair, bosom, hips, bend of legs, negligent falling hands
    all diffused, mine too diffused,

Ebb stung by the flow and flow stung by the ebb, love-flesh
    swelling and deliciously aching,
Limitless limpid jets of love hot and enormous, quivering
    jelly of love, white-blow and delirious juice,
Bridegroom night of love working surely and softly into
    the prostrate dawn,
Undulating into the willing and yielding day,
Lost in the cleave of the clasping and sweet-flesh'd day.

This the nucleus – after the child is born of woman, man
    is born of woman,
This the bath of birth, this the merge of small and large,
    and the outlet again.

Be not ashamed women, your privilege encloses the rest,
    and is the exit of the rest,
You are the gates of the body, and you are the gates of the
    soul.

The female contains all qualities and tempers them,
She is in her place and moves with perfect balance,
She is all things duly veil'd, she is both passive and active,
She is to conceive daughters as well as sons, and sons as
    well as daughters.

As I see my soul reflected in Nature,
As I see through a mist, One with inexpressible
    completeness, sanity, beauty,
See the bent head and arms folded over the breast, the
    Female I see.

6

The male is not less the soul nor more, he too is in his
    place,
He too is all qualities, he is action and power,
The flush of the known universe is in him,
Scorn becomes him well, and appetite and defiance become
    him well,
The wildest largest passions, bliss that is utmost, sorrow
    that is utmost become him well, pride is for him,
The full-spread pride of man is calming and excellent to
    the soul,
Knowledge becomes him, he likes it always, he brings
    every thing to the test of himself,
Whatever the survey, whatever the sea and the sail he
    strikes soundings at last only here,
(Where else does he strike soundings except here?)

The man's body is sacred and the woman's body is sacred,
No matter who it is, it is sacred – is it the meanest one
    in the laborers' gang?
Is it one of the dull-faced immigrants just landed on the
    wharf?

Each belongs here or anywhere just as much as the well-off,
    just as much as you,
Each has his or her place in the procession.

(All is a procession,
The universe is a procession with measured and perfect
    motion.)

Do you know so much yourself that you call the meanest
    ignorant?

Do you suppose you have a right to a good sight, and he or
   she has no right to a sight?
Do you think matter has cohered together from its diffuse
   float, and the soil is on the surface, and water runs and
   vegetation sprouts,
For you only, and not for him and her?

7

A man's body at auction,
(For before the war I often go to the slave-mart and watch
   the sale,)
I help the auctioneer, the sloven does not half know his
   business.

Gentlemen look on this wonder,
Whatever the bids of the bidders they cannot be high
   enough for it,
For it the globe lay preparing quintillions of years without
   one animal or plant,
For it the revolving cycles truly and steadily roll'd.

In this head the all-baffling brain,
In it and below it the makings of heroes.

Examine these limbs, red, black, or white, they are cunning
   in tendon and nerve,
They shall be stript that you may see them.

Exquisite senses, life-lit eyes, pluck, volition,
Flakes of breast-muscle, pliant backbone and neck, flesh
   not flabby, good-sized arms and legs,
And wonders within there yet.

Within there runs blood,
The same old blood! the same red-running blood!

There swells and jets a heart, there all passions, desires,
   reachings, aspirations,
(Do you think they are not there because they are not
   express'd in parlors and lecture-rooms?)

This is not only one man, this the father of those who shall
   be fathers in their turns,
In him the start of populous states and rich republics,
Of him countless immortal lives with countless
   embodiments and enjoyments.

How do you know who shall come from the offspring of
   his offspring through the centuries?
(Who might you find you have come from yourself, if
   you could trace back through the centuries?)

8

A woman's body at auction,
She too is not only herself, she is the teeming mother of
   mothers,
She is the bearer of them that shall grow and be mates to
   the mothers.

Have you ever loved the body of a woman?
Have you ever loved the body of a man?
Do you not see that these are exactly the same to all in
   all nations and times all over the earth?

If any thing is sacred the human body is sacred,
And the glory and sweet of a man is the token of manhood
   untainted,
And in man or woman a clean, strong, firm-fibred body,
   is more beautiful than the most beautiful face.

Have you seen the fool that corrupted his own live body?
   or the fool that corrupted her own live body?

For they do not conceal themselves, and cannot conceal
　　themselves.

9

O my body! I dare not desert the likes of you in other men
　　and women, nor the likes of the parts of you,
I believe the likes of you are to stand or fall with the likes
　　of the soul, (and that they are the soul,)
I believe the likes of you shall stand or fall with my poems,
　　and that they are my poems,
Man's, woman's, child's, youth's, wife's, husband's,
　　mother's, father's, young man's, young woman's poems,
Head, neck, hair, ears, drop and tympan of the ears,
Eyes, eye-fringes, iris of the eye, eyebrows, and the waking
　　or sleeping of the lids,
Mouth, tongue, lips, teeth, roof of the mouth, jaws, and
　　the jaw-hinges,
Nose, nostrils of the nose, and the partition,
Cheeks, temples, forehead, chin, throat, back of the neck,
　　neck-slue,
Strong shoulders, manly beard, scapula, hind-shoulders,
　　and the ample side-round of the chest,
Upper-arm, armpit, elbow-socket, lower-arm, arm-sinews,
　　arm-bones,
Wrist and wrist-joints, hand, palm, knuckles, thumb,
　　forefinger, finger-joints, finger-nails,
Broad breast-front, curling hair of the breast, breast-bone,
　　breast-side,
Ribs, belly, backbone, joints of the backbone,
Hips, hip-sockets, hip-strength, inward and outward round,
　　man-balls, man-root,
Strong set of thighs, well carrying the trunk above,
Leg-fibres, knee, knee-pan, upper-leg, under-leg,

Ankles, instep, foot-ball, toes, toe-joints, the heel;
All attitudes, all the shapeliness, all the belongings of
     my or your body or of any one's body, male or female,
The lung-sponges, the stomach-sac, the bowels sweet and
     clean,
The brain in its folds inside the skull-frame,
Sympathies, heart-valves, palate-valves, sexuality,
     maternity,
Womanhood, and all that is a woman, and the man that
     comes from woman,
The womb, the teats, nipples, breast-milk, tears, laughter,
     weeping, love-looks, love-perturbations and risings,
The voice, articulation, language, whispering, shouting
     aloud,
Food, drink, pulse, digestion, sweat, sleep, walking,
     swimming,
Poise on the hips, leaping, reclining, embracing,
     arm-curving and tightening,
The continual changes of the flex of the mouth, and
     around the eyes,
The skin, the sunburnt shade, freckles, hair,
The curious sympathy one feels when feeling with the
     hand the naked meat of the body,
The circling rivers the breath, and breathing it in and out,
The beauty of the waist, and thence of the hips, and
     thence downward toward the knees,
The thin red jellies within you or within me, the bones
     and the marrow in the bones,
The exquisite realization of health;
O I say these are not the parts and poems of the body
     only, but of the soul,
O I say now these are the soul!

1855

Spontaneous Me

Spontaneous me, Nature,
The loving day, the mounting sun, the friend I am happy
    with,
The arm of my friend hanging idly over my shoulder,
The hillside whiten'd with blossoms of the mountain ash,
The same late in autumn, the hues of red, yellow, drab,
    purple, and light and dark green,
The rich coverlet of the grass, animals and birds, the
    private untrimm'd bank, the primitive apples, the
    pebble-stones,
Beautiful dripping fragments, the negligent list of one
    after another as I happen to call them to me or think
    of them,
The real poems, (what we call poems being merely
    pictures,)
The poems of the privacy of the night, and of men like me,
This poem drooping shy and unseen that I always carry,
    and that all men carry,
(Know once for all, avow'd on purpose, wherever are men
    like me, are our lusty lurking masculine poems,)
Love-thoughts, love-juice, love-odor, love-yielding,
    love-climbers, and the climbing sap,
Arms and hands of love, lips of love, phallic thumb of
    love, breasts of love, bellies press'd and glued together
    with love,
Earth of chaste love, life that is only life after love,
The body of my love, the body of the woman I love, the
    body of the man, the body of the earth,
Soft forenoon airs that blow from the south-west,
The hairy wild-bee that murmurs and hankers up and
    down, that gripes the full-grown lady-flower, curves

upon her with amorous firm legs, takes his will of her,
and holds himself tremulous and tight till he is satisfied;
The wet of woods through the early hours,
Two sleepers at night lying close together as they sleep,
one with an arm slanting down across and below the
waist of the other,
The smell of apples, aromas from crush'd sage-plant, mint,
birch-bark,
The boy's longings, the glow and pressure as he confides
to me what he was dreaming,
The dead leaf whirling its spiral whirl and falling still
and content to the ground,
The no-form'd stings that sights, people, objects, sting
me with,
The hubb'd sting of myself, stinging me as much as it
ever can any one,
The sensitive, orbic, underlapp'd brothers, that only
privileged feelers may be intimate where they are,
The curious roamer the hand roaming all over the body,
the bashful withdrawing of flesh where the fingers
soothingly pause and edge themselves,
The limpid liquid within the young man,
The vex'd corrosion so pensive and so painful,
The torment, the irritable tide that will not be at rest,
The like of the same I feel, the like of the same in others,
The young man that flushes and flushes, and the young
woman that flushes and flushes,
The young man that wakes deep at night, the hot hand
seeking to repress what would master him,
The mystic amorous night, the strange half-welcome pangs,
visions, sweats,
The pulse pounding through palms and trembling
encircling fingers, the young man all color'd, red,
ashamed, angry;

The souse upon me of my lover the sea, as I lie willing
    and naked,
The merriment of the twin babes that crawl over the grass
    in the sun, the mother never turning her vigilant eyes
    from them,
The walnut-trunk, the walnut-husks, and the ripening or
    ripen'd long-round walnuts,
The continence of vegetables, birds, animals,
The consequent meanness of me should I skulk or find
    myself indecent, while birds and animals never once
    skulk or find themselves indecent,
The great chastity of paternity, to match the great chastity
    of maternity,
The oath of procreation I have sworn, my Adamic and
    fresh daughters,
The greed that eats me day and night with hungry gnaw,
    till I saturate what shall produce boys to fill my place
    when I am through,
The wholesome relief, repose, content,
And this bunch pluck'd at random from myself,
It has done its work – I toss it carelessly to fall where
    it may.

1856

One Hour to Madness and Joy

One hour to madness and joy! O furious! O confine me
    not!
(What is this that frees me so in storms?
What do my shouts amid lightnings and raging winds
    mean?)

O to drink the mystic deliria deeper than any other man!
O savage and tender achings! (I bequeath them to you
    my children,
I tell them to you, for reasons, O bridegroom and bride.)
O to be yielded to you whoever you are, and you to be
    yielded to me in defiance of the world!
O to return to Paradise! O bashful and feminine!
O to draw you to me, to plant on you for the first time the
    lips of a determin'd man.

O the puzzle, the thrice-tied knot, the deep and dark pool,
    all untied and illumin'd!
O to speed where there is space enough and air enough at
    last!
To be absolv'd from previous ties and conventions, I from
    mine and you from yours!
To find a new unthought-of nonchalance with the best of
    Nature!
To have the gag remov'd from one's mouth!
To have the feeling to-day or any day I am sufficient as
    I am.

O something unprov'd! something in a trance!
To escape utterly from others' anchors and holds!
To drive free! to love free! to dash reckless and dangerous!

To court destruction with taunts, with invitations!
To ascend, to leap to the heavens of the love indicated to
  me!
To rise thither with my inebriate soul!
To be lost if it must be so!
To feed the remainder of life with one hour of fulness and
  freedom!
With one brief hour of madness and joy.

1860

Scented Herbage of My Breast

Scented herbage of my breast,
Leaves from you I glean, I write, to be perused best
    afterwards,
Tomb-leaves, body-leaves growing up above me above
    death,
Perennial roots, tall leaves, O the winter shall not freeze
    you delicate leaves,
Every year shall you bloom again, out from where you
    retired you shall emerge again;
O I do not know whether many passing by will discover
    you or inhale your faint odor, but I believe a few will;
O slender leaves! O blossoms of my blood! I permit you
    to tell in your own way of the heart that is under you,
O I do not know what you mean there underneath
    yourselves, you are not happiness,
You are often more bitter than I can bear, you burn and
    sting me,
Yet you are beautiful to me you faint tinged roots, you
    make me think of death,
Death is beautiful from you, (what indeed is finally
    beautiful except death and love?)
O I think it is not for life I am chanting here my chant
    of lovers, I think it must be for death,
For how calm, how solemn it grows to ascend to the
    atmosphere of lovers,
Death or life I am then indifferent, my soul declines to
    prefer,
(I am not sure but the high soul of lovers welcomes
    death most,)
Indeed O death, I think now these leaves mean precisely
    the same as you mean,

Grow up taller sweet leaves that I may see! grow up out
of my breast!

Spring away from the conceal'd heart there!

Do not fold yourself so in your pink-tinged roots timid
leaves!

Do not remain down there so ashamed, herbage of my
breast!

Come I am determin'd to unbare this broad breast of
mine, I have long enough stifled and choked;

Emblematic and capricious blades I leave you, now you
serve me not,

I will say what I have to say by itself,

I will sound myself and comrades only, I will never again
utter a call only their call,

I will raise with it immortal reverberations through the
States,

I will give an example to lovers to take permanent shape
and will through the States,

Through me shall the words be said to make death
exhilarating,

Give me your tone therefore O death, that I may accord
with it,

Give me yourself, for I see that you belong to me now
above all, and are folded inseparably together, you love
and death are,

Nor will I allow you to balk me any more with what I was
calling life,

For now it is convey'd to me that you are the purports
essential,

That you hide in these shifting forms of life, for reasons,
and that they are mainly for you,

That you beyond them come forth to remain, the real reality,

That behind the mask of materials you patiently wait, no
matter how long,

That you will one day perhaps take control of all,
That you will perhaps dissipate this entire show of
    appearance,
That may-be you are what it is all for, but it does not last
    so very long,
But you will last very long.

1860

Of the Terrible Doubt of Appearances

Of the terrible doubt of appearances,
Of the uncertainty after all, that we may be deluded,
That may-be reliance and hope are but speculations after
    all,
That may-be identity beyond the grave is a beautiful fable
    only,
May-be the things I perceive, the animals, plants, men,
    hills, shining and flowing waters,
The skies of day and night, colors, densities, forms,
    may-be these are (as doubtless they are) only
    apparitions, and the real something has yet to be known,
(How often they dart out of themselves as if to confound
    me and mock me!
How often I think neither I know, nor any man knows,
    aught of them,)
May-be seeming to me what they are (as doubtless they
    indeed but seem) as from my present point of view, and
    might prove (as of course they would) nought of what
    they appear, or nought anyhow, from entirely changed
    points of view;
To me these and the like of these are curiously answer'd
    by my lovers, my dear friends,
When he whom I love travels with me or sits a long while
    holding me by the hand,
When the subtle air, the impalpable, the sense that words
    and reason hold not, surround us and pervade us,
Then I am charged with untold and untellable wisdom, I
    am silent, I require nothing further,

I cannot answer the question of appearances or that of
   identity beyond the grave,
But I walk or sit indifferent, I am satisfied,
He ahold of my hand has completely satisfied me.

1860

Trickle Drops

Trickle drops! my blue veins leaving!
O drops of me! trickle, slow drops,
Candid from me falling, drip, bleeding drops,
From wounds made to free you whence you were prison'd,
From my face, from my forehead and lips,
From my breast, from within where I was conceal'd, press
    forth red drops, confession drops,
Stain every page, stain every song I sing, every word I
    say, bloody drops,
Let them know your scarlet heat, let them glisten,
Saturate them with yourself all ashamed and wet,
Glow upon all I have written or shall write, bleeding
    drops,
Let it all be seen in your light, blushing drops.

1860

Here the Frailest Leaves of Me

Here the frailest leaves of me and yet my strongest lasting,
Here I shade and hide my thoughts, I myself do not
   expose them,
And yet they expose me more than all my other poems.

1860

Crossing Brooklyn Ferry

1

Flood-tide below me! I see you face to face!
Clouds of the west – sun there half an hour high – I see
you also face to face.

Crowds of men and women attired in the usual costumes,
how curious you are to me!
On the ferry-boats the hundreds and hundreds that cross,
returning home, are more curious to me than you
suppose,
And you that shall cross from shore to shore years hence
are more to me, and more in my meditations, than you
might suppose.

2

The impalpable sustenance of me from all things at all
hours of the day,
The simple, compact, well-join'd scheme, myself
disintegrated, every one disintegrated yet part of the
scheme,
The similitudes of the past and those of the future,
The glories strung like beads on my smallest sights and
hearings, on the walk in the street and the passage over
the river,
The current rushing so swiftly and swimming with me far
away,
The others that are to follow me, the ties between me and
them,
The certainty of others, the life, love, sight, hearing of
others.

Others will enter the gates of the ferry and cross from
    shore to shore,
Others will watch the run of the flood-tide,
Others will see the shipping of Manhattan north and west,
    and the heights of Brooklyn to the south and east,
Others will see the islands large and small;
Fifty years hence, others will see them as they cross, the
    sun half an hour high,
A hundred years hence, or ever so many hundred years
    hence, others will see them,
Will enjoy the sunset, the pouring-in of the flood-tide,
    the falling-back to the sea of the ebb-tide.

3

It avails not, time nor place – distance avails not,
I am with you, you men and women of a generation, or
    ever so many generations hence,
Just as you feel when you look on the river and sky, so I
    felt,
Just as any of you is one of a living crowd, I was one of a
    crowd,
Just as you are refresh'd by the gladness of the river and
    the bright flow, I was refresh'd,
Just as you stand and lean on the rail, yet hurry with the
    swift current, I stood yet was hurried,
Just as you look on the numberless masts of ships and
    the thick-stemm'd pipes of steamboats, I look'd.

I too many and many a time cross'd the river of old,
Watched the Twelfth-month sea-gulls, saw them high in
    the air floating with motionless wings, oscillating their
    bodies,
Saw how the glistening yellow lit up parts of their bodies
    and left the rest in strong shadow,

Saw the slow-wheeling circles and the gradual edging
    toward the south,
Saw the reflection of the summer sky in the water,
Had my eyes dazzled by the shimmering track of beams,
Look'd at the fine centrifugal spokes of light round the
    shape of my head in the sunlit water,
Look'd on the haze on the hills southward and
    south-westward,
Look'd on the vapor as it flew in fleeces tinged with violet,
Look'd toward the lower bay to notice the vessels arriving,
Saw their approach, saw aboard those that were near me,
Saw the white sails of schooners and sloops, saw the ships
    at anchor,
The sailors at work in the rigging or out astride the spars,
The round masts, the swinging motion of the hulls, the
    slender serpentine pennants,
The large and small steamers in motion, the pilots in their
    pilot-houses,
The white wake left by the passage, the quick tremulous
    whirl of the wheels,
The flags of all nations, the falling of them at sunset,
The scallop-edged waves in the twilight, the ladled cups,
    the frolicsome crests and glistening,
The stretch afar growing dimmer and dimmer, the gray
    walls of the granite storehouses by the docks,
On the river the shadowy group, the big steam-tug closely
    flank'd on each side by the barges, the hay-boat, the
    belated lighter,
On the neighboring shore the fires from the foundry
    chimneys burning high and glaringly into the night,
Casting their flicker of black contrasted with wild red and
    yellow light over the tops of houses, and down into the
    clefts of streets.

4

These and all else were to me the same as they are to you,
I loved well those cities, loved well the stately and rapid
    river,
The men and women I saw were all near to me,
Others the same – others who look back on me because
    I look'd forward to them,
(The time will come, though I stop here to-day and
    to-night.)

5

What is it then between us?
What is the count of the scores or hundreds of years
    between us?

Whatever it is, it avails not – distance avails not, and place
    avails not,
I too lived, Brooklyn of ample hills was mine,
I too walk'd the streets of Manhattan island, and bathed
    in the waters around it,
I too felt the curious abrupt questionings stir within me,
In the day among crowds of people sometimes they came
    upon me,
In my walks home late at night or as I lay in my bed they
    came upon me,
I too had been struck from the float forever held in
    solution,
I too had receiv'd identity by my body,
That I was I knew was of my body, and what I should be
    I knew I should be of my body.

6

It is not upon you alone the dark patches fall,
The dark threw its patches down upon me also,
The best I had done seem'd to me blank and suspicious,
My great thoughts as I supposed them, were they not in
    reality meagre?
Nor is it you alone who know what it is to be evil,
I am he who knew what it was to be evil,
I too knitted the old knot of contrariety,
Blabb'd, blush'd, resented, lied, stole, grudg'd,
Had guile, anger, lust, hot wishes I dared not speak,
Was wayward, vain, greedy, shallow, sly, cowardly,
    malignant,
The wolf, the snake, the hog, not wanting in me,
The cheating look, the frivolous word, the adulterous wish,
    not wanting,
Refusals, hates, postponements, meanness, laziness, none
    of these wanting,
Was one with the rest, the days and haps of the rest,
Was call'd by my nighest name by clear loud voices of
    young men as they saw me approaching or passing,
Felt their arms on my neck as I stood, or the negligent
    leaning of their flesh against me as I sat,
Saw many I loved in the street or ferry-boat or public
    assembly, yet never told them a word,
Lived the same life with the rest, the same old laughing,
    gnawing, sleeping,
Play'd the part that still looks back on the actor or actress,
The same old role, the role that is what we make it, as
    great as we like,
Or as small as we like, or both great and small.

7

Closer yet I approach you,
What thought you have of me now, I had as much of you
   – I laid in my stores in advance,
I consider'd long and seriously of you before you were
   born.

Who was to know what should come home to me?
Who knows but I am enjoying this?
Who knows, for all the distance, but I am as good as
   looking at you now, for all you cannot see me?

8

Ah, what can ever be more stately and admirable to me
   than mast-hemm'd Manhattan?
River and sunset and scallop-edg'd waves of flood-tide?
The sea-gulls oscillating their bodies, the hay-boat in the
   twilight, and the belated lighter?
What gods can exceed these that clasp me by the hand,
   and with voices I love call me promptly and loudly by
   my nighest name as I approach?
What is more subtle than this which ties me to the woman
   or man that looks in my face?
Which fuses me into you now, and pours my meaning into
   you?

We understand then do we not?
What I promis'd without mentioning it, have you not
   accepted?
What the study could not teach – what the preaching
   could not accomplish is accomplish'd, is it not?

9

Flow on, river! flow with the flood-tide, and ebb with the
   ebb-tide!
Frolic on, crested and scallop-edg'd waves!
Gorgeous clouds of the sunset! drench with your splendor
   me, or the men and women generations after me!
Cross from shore to shore, countless crowds of passengers!
Stand up, tall masts of Mannahatta! stand up, beautiful
   hills of Brooklyn!
Throb, baffled and curious brain! throw out questions and
   answers!
Suspend here and everywhere, eternal float of solution!
Gaze, loving and thirsty eyes, in the house or street or
   public assembly!
Sound out, voices of young men! loudly and musically
   call me by my nighest name!
Live, old life! play the part that looks back on the actor or
   actress!
Play the old role, the role that is great or small according
   as one makes it!
Consider, you who peruse me, whether I may not in
   unknown ways be looking upon you;
Be firm, rail over the river, to support those who lean idly,
   yet haste with the hasting current;
Fly on, sea-birds! fly sideways, or wheel in large circles
   high in the air;
Receive the summer sky, you water, and faithfully hold it
   till all downcast eyes have time to take it from you!
Diverge, fine spokes of light, from the shape of my head,
   or any one's head, in the sunlit water!
Come on, ships from the lower bay! pass up or down,
   white-sail'd schooners, sloops, lighters!
Flaunt away, flags of all nations! be duly lower'd at sunset!

Burn high your fires, foundry chimneys! cast black
  shadows at nightfall! cast red and yellow light over the
  tops of the houses!
Appearances, now or henceforth, indicate what you are,
You necessary film, continue to envelop the soul,
About my body for me, and your body for you, be hung
  our divinest aromas,
Thrive, cities – bring your freight, bring your shows,
  ample and sufficient rivers,
Expand, being than which none else is perhaps more
  spiritual,
Keep your places, objects than which none else is more
  lasting.

You have waited, you always wait, you dumb, beautiful
  ministers,
We receive you with free sense at last, and are insatiate
  henceforward,
Not you any more shall be able to foil us, or withhold
  yourselves from us,
We use you, and do not cast you aside – we plant you
  permanently within us,
We fathom you not – we love you – there is perfection in
  you also,
You furnish your parts toward eternity,
Great or small, you furnish your parts toward the soul.

1856

Out of the Cradle Endlessly Rocking

Out of the cradle endlessly rocking,
Out of the mocking-bird's throat, the musical shuttle,
Out of the Ninth-month midnight,
Over the sterile sands and the fields beyond, where the
     child leaving his bed wander'd alone, bareheaded,
     barefoot,
Down from the shower'd halo,
Up from the mystic play of shadows twining and twisting
     as if they were alive,
Out from the patches of briers and blackberries,
From the memories of the bird that chanted to me,
From your memories sad brother, from the fitful risings
     and fallings I heard,
From under that yellow half-moon late-risen and swollen
     as if with tears,
From those beginning notes of yearning and love there
     in the mist,
From the thousand responses of my heart never to cease,
From the myriad thence-arous'd words,
From the word stronger and more delicious than any,
From such as now they start the scene revisiting,
As a flock, twittering, rising, or overhead passing,
Borne hither, ere all eludes me, hurriedly,
A man, yet by these tears a little boy again,
Throwing myself on the sand, confronting the waves,
I, chanter of pains and joys, uniter of here and hereafter,
Taking all hints to use them, but swiftly leaping beyond
     them,
A reminiscence sing.

Once Paumanok,
When the lilac-scent was in the air and Fifth-month grass
    was growing,
Up this seashore in some briers,
Two feather'd guests from Alabama, two together,
And their nest, and four light-green eggs spotted with
    brown,
And every day the he-bird to and fro near at hand,
And every day the she-bird crouch'd on her nest, silent,
    with bright eyes,
And every day I, a curious boy, never too close, never
    disturbing them,
Cautiously peering, absorbing, translating.

Shine! shine! shine!
Pour down your warmth, great sun!
While we bask, we two together.

Two together!
Winds blow south, or winds blow north,
Day come white, or night come black,
Home, or rivers and mountains from home,
Singing all time, minding no time,
While we two keep together.

Till of a sudden,
May-be kill'd, unknown to her mate,
One forenoon the she-bird crouch'd not on the nest,
Nor return'd that afternoon, nor the next,
Nor ever appear'd again.

And thenceforward all summer in the sound of the sea,
And at night under the full of the moon in calmer weather,
Over the hoarse surging of the sea,

Or flitting from brier to brier by day,
I saw, I heard at intervals the remaining one, the he-bird
The solitary guest from Alabama.

Blow! blow! blow!
Blow up sea-winds along Paumanok's shore;
I wait and I wait till you blow my mate to me.

Yes, when the stars glisten'd,
All night long on the prong of a moss-scallop'd stake,
Down almost amid the slapping waves,
Sat the lone singer wonderful causing tears.

He call'd on his mate,
He pour'd forth the meanings which I of all men know.

Yes my brother I know,
The rest might not, but I have treasur'd every note,
For more than once dimly down to the beach gliding,
Silent, avoiding the moonbeams, blending myself with the
    shadows,
Recalling now the obscure shapes, the echoes, the sounds
    and sights after their sorts,
The white arms out in the breakers tirelessly tossing,
I, with bare feet, a child, the wind wafting my hair,
Listen'd long and long.

Listen'd to keep, to sing, now translating the notes,
Following you my brother.

Soothe! soothe! soothe!
Close on its wave soothes the wave behind,
And again another behind embracing and lapping, every one
    close,
But my love soothes not me, not me.

Low hangs the moon, it rose late,
It is lagging – O I think it is heavy with love, with love.

O madly the sea pushes upon the land,
With love, with love.

O night! do I not see my love fluttering out among the
  breakers?
What is that little black thing I see there in the white?

Loud! loud! loud!
Loud I call to you, my love!

High and clear I shoot my voice over the waves,
Surely you must know who is here, is here,
You must know who I am, my love.

Low-hanging moon!
What is that dusky spot in your brown yellow?
O it is the shape, the shape of my mate!
O moon do not keep her from me any longer.

Land! land! O land!
Whichever way I turn, O I think you could give me my mate
  back again if you only would,
For I am almost sure I see her dimly whichever way I look.

O rising stars!
Perhaps the one I want so much will rise, will rise with some
  of you.

O throat! O trembling throat!
Sound clearer through the atmosphere!
Pierce the woods, the earth,
Somewhere listening to catch you must be the one I want.

Shake out carols!
Solitary here, the night's carols!
Carols of lonesome love! death's carols!
Carols under that lagging, yellow, waning moon!
O under that moon where she droops almost down into the sea!
O reckless despairing carols.

But soft! sink low!
Soft! let me just murmur,
And do you wait a moment you husky-nois'd sea,
For somewhere I believe I heard my mate responding to me,
So faint, I must be still, be still to listen,
But not altogether still, for then she might not come
    immediately to me.

Hither my love!
Here I am! here!
With this just-sustain'd note I announce myself to you,
This gentle call is for you my love, for you.

Do not be decoy'd elsewhere,
That is the whistle of the wind, it is not my voice,
That is the fluttering, the fluttering of the spray,
Those are the shadows of leaves.

O darkness! O in vain!
O I am very sick and sorrowful.

O brown halo in the sky near the moon, drooping upon the
    sea!
O troubled reflection in the sea!
O throat! O throbbing heart!
And I singing uselessly, uselessly all the night.

O past! O happy life! O songs of joy!
In the air, in the woods, over fields,
Loved! loved! loved! loved! loved!
But my mate no more, no more with me!
We two together no more.

The aria sinking,
All else continuing, the stars shining,
The winds blowing, the notes of the bird continuous
    echoing,
With angry moans the fierce old mother incessantly
    moaning,
On the sands of Paumanok's shore gray and rustling,
The yellow half-moon enlarged, sagging down, drooping,
    the face of the sea almost touching,
The boy ecstatic, with his bare feet the waves, with his
    hair the atmosphere dallying,
The love in the heart long pent, now loose, now at last
    tumultuously bursting,
The aria's meaning, the ears, the soul, swiftly depositing,
The strange tears down the cheeks coursing,
The colloquy there, the trio, each uttering,
The undertone, the savage old mother incessantly crying,
To the boy's soul's questions sullenly timing, some drown'd
    secret hissing,
To the outsetting bard.

Demon or bird! (said the boy's soul,)
Is it indeed toward your mate you sing? or is it really to
    me?
For I, that was a child, my tongue's use sleeping, now I
    have heard you,
Now in a moment I know what I am for, I awake,

And already a thousand singers, a thousand songs, clearer,
    louder and more sorrowful than yours,
A thousand warbling echoes have started to life within
    me, never to die.

O you singer solitary, singing by yourself, projecting me,
O solitary me listening, never more shall I cease
    perpetuating you,
Never more shall I escape, never more the reverberations,
Never more the cries of unsatisfied love be absent from me,
Never again leave me to be the peaceful child I was before
    what there in the night,
By the sea under the yellow and sagging moon,
The messenger there arous'd, the fire, the sweet hell
    within,
The unknown want, the destiny of me.

O give me the clew! (it lurks in the night here somewhere,)
O if I am to have so much, let me have more!

A word then, (for I will conquer it,)
The word final, superior to all,
Subtle, sent up – what is it? – I listen;
Are you whispering it, and have been all the time, you
    sea-waves?
Is that it from your liquid rims and wet sands?

Whereto answering, the sea,
Delaying not, hurrying not,
Whisper'd me through the night, and very plainly before
    daybreak,
Lisp'd to me the low and delicious word death,
And again death, death, death, death,

Hissing melodious, neither like the bird nor like my
    arous'd child's heart,
But edging near as privately for me rustling at my feet,
Creeping thence steadily up to my ears and laving me
    softly all over,
Death, death, death, death, death.

Which I do not forget,
But fuse the song of my dusky demon and brother,
That he sang to me in the moonlight on Paumanok's gray
    beach,
With the thousand responsive songs at random,
My own songs awaked from that hour,
And with them the key, the word up from the waves,
The word of the sweetest song and all songs,
That strong and delicious word which, creeping to my feet,
(Or like some old crone rocking the cradle, swathed in
    sweet garments, bending aside,)
The sea whisper'd me.

1859

As I Ebb'd with the Ocean of Life

I

As I ebb'd with the ocean of life,
As I wended the shores I know,
As I walk'd where the ripples continually wash you
    Paumanok,
Where they rustle up hoarse and sibilant,
Where the fierce old mother endlessly cries for her
    castaways,
I musing late in the autumn day, gazing off southward,
Held by this electric self out of the pride of which I utter
    poems,
Was seiz'd by the spirit that trails in the lines underfoot,
The rim, the sediment that stands for all the water and all
    the land of the globe.

Fascinated, my eyes reverting from the south, dropt, to
    follow those slender windrows,
Chaff, straw, splinters of wood, weeds, and the sea-gluten,
Scum, scales from shining rocks, leaves of salt-lettuce, left
    by the tide,
Miles walking, the sound of breaking waves the other side
    of me,
Paumanok there and then as I thought the old thought of
    likenesses,
These you presented to me you fish-shaped island,
As I wended the shores I know,
As I walk'd with that electric self seeking types.

2

As I wend to the shores I know not,
As I list to the dirge, the voices of men and women
 wreck'd,
As I inhale the impalpable breezes that set in upon me,
As the ocean so mysterious rolls toward me closer and
 closer,
I too but signify at the utmost a little wash'd-up drift,
A few sands and dead leaves to gather,
Gather, and merge myself as part of the sands and drift.

O baffled, balk'd, bent to the very earth,
Oppress'd with myself that I have dared to open my
 mouth,
Aware now that amid all that blab whose echoes recoil
 upon me I have not once had the least idea who or
 what I am,
But that before all my arrogant poems the real Me stands
 yet untouch'd, untold, altogether unreach'd,
Withdrawn far, mocking me with mock-congratulatory
 signs and bows,
With peals of distant ironical laughter at every word I
 have written,
Pointing in silence to these songs, and then to the sand
 beneath.

I perceive I have not really understood any thing, not a
 single object, and that no man ever can,
Nature here in sight of the sea taking advantage of me to
 dart upon me and sting me,
Because I have dared to open my mouth to sing at all.

3

You oceans both, I close with you,
We murmur alike reproachfully rolling sands and drift,
   knowing not why,
These little shreds instead standing for you and me and all.

You friable shore with trails of debris,
You fish-shaped island, I take what is underfoot,
What is yours is mine my father.

I too Paumanok,
I too have bubbled up, floated the measureless float, and
   been wash'd on your shores,
I too am but a trail of drift and debris,
I too leave little wrecks upon you, you fish-shaped island.

I throw myself upon your breast my father,
I cling to you so that you cannot unloose me,
I hold you so firm till you answer me something.

Kiss me my father,
Touch me with your lips as I touch those I love,
Breathe to me while I hold you close the secret of the
   murmuring I envy.

4

Ebb, ocean of life, (the flow will return,)
Cease not your moaning you fierce old mother,
Endlessly cry for your castaways, but fear not, deny not
   me,
Rustle not up so hoarse and angry against my feet as I
   touch you or gather from you.

I mean tenderly by you and all,
I gather for myself and for this phantom looking down where
   we lead, and following me and mine.

Me and mine, loose windrows, little corpses,
Froth, snowy white, and bubbles,
(See, from my dead lips the ooze exuding at last,
See, the prismatic colors glistening and rolling,)
Tufts of straw, sands, fragments,
Buoy'd hither from many moods, one contradicting
   another,
From the storm, the long calm, the darkness, the swell,
Musing, pondering, a breath, a briny tear, a dab of liquid
   or soil,
Up just as much out of fathomless workings fermented
   and thrown,
A limp blossom or two, torn, just as much over waves
   floating, drifted at random,
Just as much for us that sobbing dirge of Nature,
Just as much whence we come that blare of the
   cloud-trumpets,
We, capricious, brought hither we know not whence,
   spread out before you,
You up there walking or sitting,
Whoever you are, we too lie in drifts at your feet.

1860

A Boston Ballad

To get betimes in Boston town I rose this morning early,
Here's a good place at the corner, I must stand and see
   the show.

Clear the way there Jonathan!
Way for the President's marshal – way for the government
   cannon!
Way for the Federal foot and dragoons, (and the
   apparitions copiously tumbling.)

I love to look on the Stars and Stripes, I hope the fifes
   will play Yankee Doodle.
How bright shine the cutlasses of the foremost troops!
Every man holds his revolver, marching stiff through
   Boston town.

A fog follows, antiques of the same come limping,
Some appear wooden-legged, and some appear bandaged
   and bloodless.

Why this is indeed a show – it has called the dead out of
   the earth!
The old graveyards of the hills have hurried to see!

Phantoms! phantoms countless by flank and rear!
Cock'd hats of mothy mould – crutches made of mist!
Arms in slings – old men leaning on young men's
   shoulders.

What troubles you Yankee phantoms? what is all this
   chattering of bare gums?
Does the ague convulse your limbs? do you mistake your
   crutches for firelocks and level them?

If you blind your eyes with tears you will not see the
    President's marshal,
If you groan such groans you might balk the government
    cannon.

For shame old maniacs – bring down those toss'd arms,
    and let your white hair be,
Here gape your great grandsons, their wives gaze at them
    from the windows,
See how well dress'd, see how orderly they conduct
    themselves.

Worse and worse – can't you stand it? are you retreating?
Is this hour with the living too dead for you?

Retreat then – pell-mell!
To your graves – back – back to the hills old limpers!
I do not think you belong here anyhow.

But there is one thing that belongs here – shall I tell you
    what it is, gentlemen of Boston?

I will whisper it to the Mayor, he shall send a committee
    to England,
They shall get a grant from the Parliament, go with a cart
    to the royal vault,
Dig out King George's coffin, unwrap him quick from the
    grave-clothes, box up his bones for a journey,
Find a swift Yankee clipper – here is freight for you,
    black-bellied clipper,
Up with your anchor – shake out your sails – steer straight
    toward Boston bay.

Now call for the President's marshal again, bring out the
  government cannon,
Fetch home the roarers from Congress, make another
  procession, guard it with foot and dragoons.

This centre-piece for them;
Look, all orderly citizens – look from the windows,
  women!

The committee open the box, set up the regal ribs, glue
  those that will not stay,
Clap the skull on top of the ribs, and clap a crown on top
  of the skull.

You have got your revenge, old buster – the crown is come
  to its own, and more than its own.

Stick your hands in your pockets, Jonathan – you are a
  made man from this day,
You are mighty cute – and here is one of your bargains.

1854

A Hand-Mirror

Hold it up sternly – see this it sends back, (who is it? is it
    you?)
Outside fair costume, within ashes and filth,
No more a flashing eye, no more a sonorous voice or
    springy step,
Now some slave's eye, voice, hands, step,
A drunkard's breath, unwholesome eater's face,
    venerealee's flesh,
Lungs rotting away piecemeal, stomach sour and
    cankerous,
Joints rheumatic, bowels clogged with abomination,
Blood circulating dark and poisonous streams,
Words babble, hearing and touch callous,
No brain, no heart left, no magnetism of sex;
Such from one look in this looking-glass ere you go hence,
Such a result so soon – and from such a beginning!

1860

Germs

Forms, qualities, lives, humanity, language, thoughts,
The ones known, and the ones unknown, the ones on the
stars,
The stars themselves, some shaped, others unshaped,
Wonders as of those countries, the soil, trees, cities,
inhabitants, whatever they may be,
Splendid suns, the moon and rings, the countless
combinations and effects,
Such-like, and as good as such-like, visible here or
anywhere, stand provided for in a handful of space,
which I extend my arm and half enclose with my hand,
That containing the start of each and all, the virtue, the
germs of all.

1860

Perfections

Only themselves understand themselves and the like of
    themselves,
As souls only understand souls.

1860

Vigil Strange I Kept on the Field One Night

Vigil strange I kept on the field one night;
When you and my son and my comrade dropt at my side
    that day,
One look I but gave which your dear eyes return'd with a
    look I shall never forget,
One touch of your hand to mine O boy, reach'd up as you
    lay on the ground,
Then onward I sped in the battle, the even-contested battle,
Till late in the night reliev'd to the place at last again I
    made my way,
Found you in death so cold dear comrade, found your
    body son of responding kisses, (never again on earth
    responding,)
Bared your face in the starlight, curious the scene, cool
    blew the moderate night-wind,
Long there and then in vigil I stood, dimly around me
    the battlefield spreading,
Vigil wondrous and vigil sweet there in the fragrant silent
    night,
But not a tear fell, not even a long-drawn sigh, long, long
    I gazed,
Then on the earth partially reclining sat by your side
    leaning my chin in my hands,
Passing sweet hours, immortal and mystic hours with you
    dearest comrade – not a tear, not a word,
Vigil of silence, love and death, vigil for you my son and
    my soldier,
As onward silently stars aloft, eastward new ones upward
    stole,

Vigil final for you brave boy, (I could not save you, swift
    was your death,
I faithfully loved you and cared for you living, I think we
    shall surely meet again,)
Till at latest lingering of the night, indeed just as the dawn
    appear'd,
My comrade I wrapt in his blanket, envelop'd well his
    form,
Folded the blanket well, tucking it carefully over head and
    carefully under feet,
And there and then and bathed by the rising sun, my son
    in his grave, in his rude-dug grave I deposited,
Ending my vigil strange with that, vigil of night and
    battle-field dim,
Vigil for boy of responding kisses, (never again on earth
    responding,)
Vigil for comrade swiftly slain, vigil I never forget, how as
    day brighten'd,
I rose from the chill ground and folded my soldier well in
    his blanket,
And buried him where he fell.

1865

The Wound-Dresser

1

An old man bending I come among new faces,
Years looking backward resuming in answer to children,
Come tell us old man, as from young men and maidens
    that love me,
(Arous'd and angry, I'd thought to beat the alarum, and
    urge relentless war,
But soon my fingers fail'd me, my face droop'd and I
    resign'd myself,
To sit by the wounded and soothe them, or silently watch
    the dead;)
Years hence of these scenes, of these furious passions,
    these chances,
Of unsurpass'd heroes, (was one side so brave? the other
    was equally brave;)
Now be witness again, paint the mightiest armies of earth,
Of those armies so rapid so wondrous what saw you to tell
    us?
What stays with you latest and deepest? of curious panics,
Of hard-fought engagements or sieges tremendous what
    deepest remains?

2

O maidens and young men I love and that love me,
What you ask of my days those the strangest and sudden
    your talking recalls,
Soldier alert I arrive after a long march cover'd with sweat
    and dust,
In the nick of time I come, plunge in the fight, loudly shout
    in the rush of successful charge

Enter the captur'd works – yet lo, like a swift-running river
they fade,
Pass and are gone they fade – I dwell not on soldiers' perils
or soldiers' joys,
(Both I remember well – many the hardships, few the joys,
yet I was content.)

But in silence, in dreams' projections,
While the world of gain and appearance and mirth goes on,
So soon what is over forgotten, and waves wash the
imprints off the sand,
With hinged knees returning I enter the doors, (while for
you up there,
Whoever you are, follow without noise and be of strong
heart.)

Bearing the bandages, water and sponge,
Straight and swift to my wounded I go,
Where they lie on the ground after the battle brought in,
Where their priceless blood reddens the grass the ground,
Or to the rows of the hospital tent, or under the roof'd
hospital,
To the long rows of cots up and down each side I return,
To each and all one after another I draw near, not one do
I miss,
An attendant follows holding a tray, he carries a refuse pail,
Soon to be fill'd with clotted rags and blood, emptied, and
fill'd again.

I onward go, I stop,
With hinged knees and steady hand to dress wounds,
I am firm with each, the pangs are sharp yet unavoidable,

One turns to me his appealing eyes – poor boy! I never
  knew you,
Yet I think I could not refuse this moment to die for you,
  if that would save you.

3

On, on I go, (open doors of time! open hospital doors!)
The crush'd head I dress, (poor crazed hand tear not the
  bandage away,)
The neck of the cavalry-man with the bullet through and
  through I examine,
Hard the breathing rattles, quite glazed already the eye,
  yet life struggles hard,
(Come sweet death! be persuaded O beautiful death!
In mercy come quickly.)

From the stump of the arm, the amputated hand,
I undo the clotted lint, remove the slough, wash off the
  matter and blood,
Back on his pillow the soldier bends with curv'd neck and
  side-falling head,
His eyes are closed, his face is pale, he dares not look on
  the bloody stump,
And has not yet look'd on it.

I dress a wound in the side, deep, deep,
But a day or two more, for see the frame all wasted and
  sinking,
And the yellow-blue countenance see.

I dress the perforated shoulder, the foot with the
  bullet-wound,

Cleanse the one with a gnawing and putrid gangrene, so
    sickening, so offensive,
While the attendant stands behind aside me holding the
    tray and pail.

I am faithful, I do not give out,
The fractur'd thigh, the knee, the wound in the abdomen,
These and more I dress with impassive hand, (yet deep
    in my breast a fire, a burning flame.)

4

Thus in silence in dreams' projections,
Returning, resuming, I thread my way through the
    hospitals,
The hurt and wounded I pacify with soothing hand,
I sit by the restless all the dark night, some are so young,
Some suffer so much, I recall the experience sweet and
    sad,
(Many a soldier's loving arms about this neck have cross'd
    and rested,
Many a soldier's kiss dwells on these bearded lips.)

1865

Reconciliation

Word over all, beautiful as the sky,
Beautiful that war and all its deeds of carnage must in
   time be utterly lost,
That the hands of the sisters Death and Night incessantly
   softly wash again, and ever again, this soil'd world;
For my enemy is dead, a man divine as myself is dead,
I look where he lies white-faced and still in the coffin – I
   draw near,
Bend down and touch lightly with my lips the white face
   in the coffin.

1865–6

When Lilacs Last in the Dooryard Bloom'd

1

When lilacs last in the dooryard bloom'd,
And the great star early droop'd in the western sky in the
   night,
I mourn'd, and yet shall mourn with ever-returning spring.

Ever-returning spring, trinity sure to me you bring,
Lilac blooming perennial and drooping star in the west,
And thought of him I love.

2

O powerful western fallen star!
O shades of night – O moody, tearful night!
O great star disappear'd – O the black murk that hides
   the star!
O cruel hands that hold me powerless – O helpless soul
   of me!
O harsh surrounding cloud that will not free my soul.

3

In the dooryard fronting an old farm-house near the
   white-wash'd palings,
Stands the lilac-bush tall-growing with heart-shaped leaves
   of rich green,
With many a pointed blossom rising delicate, with the
   perfume strong I love,
With every leaf a miracle – and from this bush in the
   dooryard,
With delicate-color'd blossoms and heart-shaped leaves
   of rich green,
A sprig with its flower I break.

4

In the swamp in secluded recesses,
A shy and hidden bird is warbling a song.

Solitary the thrush,
The hermit withdrawn to himself, avoiding the settlements,
Sings by himself a song.

Song of the bleeding throat,
Death's outlet song of life, (for well dear brother I know,
If thou wast not granted to sing thou would'st surely die.)

5

Over the breast of the spring, the land, amid cities,
Amid lanes and through old woods, where lately the violets
    peep'd from the ground, spotting the gray debris,
Amid the grass in the fields each side of the lanes, passing
    the endless grass,
Passing the yellow-spear'd wheat, every grain from its
    shroud in the dark-brown fields uprisen,
Passing the apple-tree blows of white and pink in the
    orchards,
Carrying a corpse to where it shall rest in the grave,
Night and day journeys a coffin.

6

Coffin that passes through lanes and streets,
Through day and night with the great cloud darkening
    the land,
With the pomp of the inloop'd flags with the cities draped
    in black,

With the show of the States themselves as of crape-veil'd
    women standing,
With processions long and winding and the flambeaus
    of the night,
With the countless torches lit, with the silent sea of faces
    and the unbared heads,
With the waiting depot, the arriving coffin, and the sombre
    faces,
With dirges through the night, with the thousand voices
    rising strong and solemn,
With all the mournful voices of the dirges pour'd around
    the coffin,
The dim-lit churches and the shuddering organs – where
    amid these you journey,
With the tolling tolling bells' perpetual clang,
Here, coffin that slowly passes,
I give you my sprig of lilac.

7

(Nor for you, for one alone,
Blossoms and branches green to coffins all I bring,
For fresh as the morning, thus would I chant a song for
    you O sane and sacred death.

All over bouquets of roses,
O death, I cover you over with roses and early lilies,
But mostly and now the lilac that blooms the first,
Copious I break, I break the sprigs from the bushes,
With loaded arms I come, pouring for you,
For you and the coffins all of you O death.)

8

O western orb sailing the heaven,
Now I know what you must have meant as a month since
　I walk'd,
As I walk'd in silence the transparent shadowy night,
As I saw you had something to tell as you bent to me
　night after night,
As you droop'd from the sky low down as if to my side,
　(while the other stars all look'd on,)
As we wander'd together the solemn night, (for something
　I know not what kept me from sleep,)
As the night advanced, and I saw on the rim of the west
　how full you were of woe,
As I stood on the rising ground in the breeze in the cool
　transparent night,
As I watch'd where you pass'd and was lost in the
　netherward black of the night,
As my soul in its trouble dissatisfied sank, as where you
　sad orb,
Concluded, dropt in the night, and was gone.

9

Sing on there in the swamp,
O singer bashful and tender, I hear your notes, I hear
　your call,
I hear, I come presently, I understand you,
But a moment I linger, for the lustrous star has detain'd
　me,
The star my departing comrade holds and detains me.

10

O how shall I warble myself for the dead one there I
    loved?
And how shall I deck my song for the large sweet soul
    that has gone?
And what shall my perfume be for the grave of him I love?

Sea-winds blown from east and west,
Blown from the Eastern sea and blown from the Western
    sea, till there on the prairies meeting,
These and with these and the breath of my chant,
I'll perfume the grave of him I love.

11

O what shall I hang on the chamber walls?
And what shall the pictures be that I hang on the walls,
To adorn the burial-house of him I love?

Pictures of growing spring and farms and homes,
With the Fourth-month eve at sundown, and the gray
    smoke lucid and bright,
With floods of the yellow gold of the gorgeous, indolent,
    sinking sun, burning, expanding the air,
With the fresh sweet herbage under foot, and the pale
    green leaves of the trees prolific,
In the distance the flowing glaze, the breast of the river,
    with a wind-dapple here and there,
With ranging hills on the banks, with many a line against
    the sky, and shadows,
And the city at hand with dwellings so dense, and stacks
    of chimneys,
And all the scenes of life and the workshops, and the
    workmen homeward returning.

12

Lo, body and soul – this land,
My own Manhattan with spires, and the sparkling and
   hurrying tides, and the ships,
The varied and ample land, the South and the North in
   the light, Ohio's shores and flashing Missouri,
And ever the far-spreading prairies cover'd with grass and
   corn.

Lo, the most excellent sun so calm and haughty,
The violet and purple morn with just-felt breezes,
The gentle soft-born measureless light,
The miracle spreading bathing all, the fulfill'd noon,
The coming eve delicious, the welcome night and the stars,
Over my cities shining all, enveloping man and land.

13

Sing on, sing on you gray-brown bird,
Sing from the swamps, the recesses, pour your chant from
   the bushes,
Limitless out of the dusk, out of the cedars and pines.

Sing on dearest brother, warble your reedy song,
Loud human song, with voice of uttermost woe.

O liquid and free and tender!
O wild and loose to my soul – O wondrous singer!
You only I hear – yet the star holds me, (but will soon
   depart,)
Yet the lilac with mastering odor holds me.

14

Now while I sat in the day and look'd forth,
In the close of the day with its light and the fields of
    spring, and the farmers preparing their crops,
In the large unconscious scenery of my land with its lakes
    and forests,
In the heavenly aerial beauty, (after the perturb'd winds
    and the storms,)
Under the arching heavens of the afternoon swift passing,
    and the voices of children and women,
The man-moving sea-tides, and I saw the ships how they
    sail'd,
And the summer approaching with richness, and the fields
    all busy with labor,
And the infinite separate houses, how they all went on,
    each with its meals and minutia of daily usages,
And the streets how their throbbings throbb'd, and the
    cities pent – lo, then and there,
Falling upon them all and among them all, enveloping me
    with the rest,
Appear'd the cloud, appear'd the long black trail,
And I knew death, its thought, and the sacred knowledge
    of death.

Then with the knowledge of death as walking one side of
    me,
And the thought of death close-walking the other side of me,
And I in the middle as with companions, and as holding
    the hands of companions,
I fled forth to the hiding receiving night that talks not,
Down to the shores of the water, the path by the swamp
    in the dimness,
To the solemn shadowy cedars and ghostly pines so still.

And the singer so shy to the rest receiv'd me,
The gray-brown bird I know receiv'd us comrades three,
And he sang the carol of death, and a verse for him I love.

From deep secluded recesses,
From the fragrant cedars and the ghostly pines so still,
Came the carol of the bird.

And the charm of the carol rapt me,
As I held as if by their hands my comrades in the night,
And the voice of my spirit tallied the song of the bird.

Come lovely and soothing death,
Undulate round the world, serenely arriving, arriving,
In the day, in the night, to all, to each,
Sooner or later delicate death.

Prais'd be the fathomless universe,
For life and joy, and for objects and knowledge curious,
And for love, sweet love – but praise! praise! praise!
For the sure-enwinding arms of cool-enfolding death.

Dark mother always gliding near with soft feet,
Have none chanted for thee a chant of fullest welcome?
Then I chant it for thee, I glorify thee above all,
I bring thee a song that when thou must indeed come, come
   unfalteringly.

Approach strong deliveress,
When it is so, when thou hast taken them I joyously sing the
   dead,
Lost in the loving floating ocean of thee,
Laved in the flood of thy bliss O death.

From me to thee glad serenades,
Dances for thee I propose saluting thee, adornments and
*   feastings for thee,*
And the sights of the open landscape and the high-spread
*   sky are fitting,*
And life and the fields, and the huge and thoughtful night.

The night in silence under many a star,
The ocean shore and the husky whispering wave whose voice
*   I know,*
And the soul turning to thee O vast and well-veil'd death,
And the body gratefully nestling close to thee.

Over the tree-tops I float thee a song,
Over the rising and sinking waves, over the myriad fields
*   and the prairies wide,*
Over the dense-pack'd cities all and the teeming wharves
*   and ways,*
I float this carol with joy, with joy to thee O death.

15

To the tally of my soul,
Loud and strong kept up the gray-brown bird,
With pure deliberate notes spreading filling the night.

Loud in the pines and cedars dim,
Clear in the freshness moist and the swamp-perfume,
And I with my comrades there in the night.

While my sight that was found in my eyes unclosed,
As to long panoramas of visions.

And I saw askant the armies,
I saw as in noiseless dreams hundreds of battle-flags,

Borne through the smoke of the battles and pierc'd with
    missiles I saw them,
And carried hither and yon through the smoke, and torn
    and bloody,
And at last but a few shreds left on the staff, (and all in
    silence,)
And the staffs all splinter'd and broken.

I saw battle-corpses, myriads of them,
And the white skeletons of young men, I saw them,
I saw the debris and debris of all the slain soldiers of the
    war,
But I saw they were not as was thought,
They themselves were fully at rest, they suffer'd not,
The living remain'd and suffer'd, the mother suffer'd,
And the wife and the child and the musing comrade
    suffer'd,
And the armies that remain'd suffer'd.

16

Passing the visions, passing the night,
Passing, unloosing the hold of my comrades' hands,
Passing the song of the hermit bird and the tallying song
    of my soul,
Victorious song, death's outlet song, yet varying,
    ever-altering song,
As low and wailing, yet clear the notes, rising and falling,
    flooding the night,
Sadly sinking and fainting, as warning and warning, and
    yet again bursting with joy,
Covering the earth and filling the spread of the heaven,
As that powerful psalm in the night I heard from recesses,
Passing, I leave thee lilac with heart-shaped leaves,

I leave thee there in the door-yard, blooming, returning
　with spring.

I cease from my song for thee,
From my gaze on thee in the west, fronting the west,
　communing with thee,
O comrade lustrous with silver face in the night.

Yet each to keep and all, retrievements out of the night,
The song, the wondrous chant of the gray-brown bird,
And the tallying chant, the echo arous'd in my soul,
With the lustrous and drooping star with the countenance
　full of woe,
With the holders holding my hand nearing the call of the
　bird,
Comrades mine and I in the midst, and their memory
　ever to keep, for the dead I loved so well,
For the sweetest, wisest soul of all my days and lands –
　and this for his dear sake,
Lilac and star and bird twined with the chant of my soul,
There in the fragrant pines and the cedars dusk and dim.

1865–6

By Blue Ontario's Shore

1

By blue Ontario's shore,
As I mused of these warlike days and of peace return'd,
    and the dead that return no more,
A Phantom gigantic superb, with stern visage accosted me,
Chant me the poem, it said, *that comes from the soul of
    America, chant me the carol of victory,*
*And strike up the marches of Libertad, marches more powerful
    yet,*
*And sing me before you go the song of the throes of
    Democracy.*

(Democracy, the destin'd conqueror, yet treacherous
    lip-smiles everywhere,
And death and infidelity at every step.)

2

A Nation announcing itself,
I myself make the only growth by which I can be
    appreciated,
I reject none, accept all, then reproduce all in my own
    forms.

A breed whose proof is in time and deeds,
What we are we are, nativity is answer enough to
    objections,
We wield ourselves as a weapon is wielded,
We are powerful and tremendous in ourselves,
We are executive in ourselves, we are sufficient in the
    variety of ourselves,

We are the most beautiful to ourselves and in ourselves,
We stand self-pois'd in the middle, branching thence over
    the world,
From Missouri, Nebraska, or Kansas, laughing attacks to
    scorn.

Nothing is sinful to us outside of ourselves,
Whatever appears, whatever does not appear, we are
    beautiful or sinful in ourselves only.

(O Mother – O Sisters dear!
If we are lost, no victor else has destroy'd us,
It is by ourselves we go down to eternal night.)

3

Have you thought there could be but a single supreme?
There can be any number of supremes – one does not
    countervail another any more than one eyesight
    countervails another, or one life countervails another.

All is eligible to all,
All is for individuals, all is for you,
No condition is prohibited, not God's or any.

All comes by the body, only health puts you rapport with
    the universe.

Produce great Persons, the rest follows.

4

Piety and conformity to them that like,
Peace, obesity, allegiance, to them that like,
I am he who tauntingly compels men, women, nations,
Crying, Leap from your seats and contend for your lives!

I am he who walks the States with a barb'd tongue,
  questioning every one I meet,
Who are you that wanted only to be told what you knew
  before?
Who are you that wanted only a book to join you in your
  nonsense?

(With pangs and cries as thine own O bearer of many
  children,
These clamors wild to a race of pride I give.)

O lands, would you be freer than all that has ever been
  before?
If you would be freer than all that has been before, come
  listen to me.

Fear grace, elegance, civilization, delicatesse,
Fear the mellow sweet, the sucking of honey-juice,
Beware the advancing mortal ripening of Nature,
Beware what precedes the decay of the ruggedness of states
  and men.

5

Ages, precedents, have long been accumulating undirected
  materials,
America brings builders, and brings its own styles.

The immortal poets of Asia and Europe have done their
  work and pass'd to other spheres,
A work remains, the work of surpassing all they have done.

America, curious toward foreign characters, stands by its
  own at all hazards,
Stands removed, spacious, composite, sound, initiates the
  true use of precedents,

Does not repel them or the past or what they have
    produced under their forms,
Takes the lesson with calmness, perceives the corpse
    slowly borne from the house,
Perceives that it waits a little while in the door, that it
    was fittest for its days,
That its life has descended to the stalwart and well-shaped
    heir who approaches,
And that he shall be fittest for his days.

Any period one nation must lead,
One land must be the promise and reliance of the future.

These States are the amplest poem,
Here is not merely a nation but a teeming Nation of
    nations,
Here the doings of men correspond with the broadcast
    doings of the day and night,
Here is what moves in magnificent masses careless of
    particulars,
Here are the roughs, beards, friendliness, combativeness,
    the soul loves,
Here the flowing trains, here the crowds, equality, diversity,
    the soul loves.

6

Land of lands and bards to corroborate!
Of them standing among them, one lifts to the light a
    west-bred face,
To him the hereditary countenance bequeath'd both
    mother's and father's,
His first parts substances, earth, water, animals, trees,
Built of the common stock, having room for far and near,

Used to dispense with other lands, incarnating this land,
Attracting it body and soul to himself, hanging on its
    neck with incomparable love,
Plunging his seminal muscle into its merits and demerits,
Making its cities, beginnings, events, diversities, wars,
    vocal in him,
Making its rivers, lakes, bays, embouchure in him,
Mississippi with yearly freshets and changing chutes,
    Columbia, Niagara, Hudson, spending themselves
    lovingly in him,
If the Atlantic coast stretch or the Pacific coast stretch,
    he stretching with them North or South,
Spanning between them East and West, and touching
    whatever is between them,
Growths growing from him to offset the growths of pine,
    cedar, hemlock, live-oak, locust, chestnut, hickory,
    cottonwood, orange, magnolia,
Tangles as tangled in him as any canebrake or swamp,
He likening sides and peaks of mountains, forests coated
    with northern transparent ice,
Off him pasturage sweet and natural as savanna, upland,
    prairie,
Through him flights, whirls, screams, answering those of
    the fish-hawk, mocking-bird, night-heron, and eagle,
His spirit surrounding his country's spirit, unclosed to
    good and evil,
Surrounding the essences of real things, old times and
    present times,
Surrounding just found shores, islands, tribes of red
    aborigines,
Weather-beaten vessels, landings, settlements, embryo
    stature and muscle,
The haughty defiance of the Year One, war, peace, the
    formation of the Constitution,

The separate States, the simple elastic scheme, the
  immigrants,
The Union always swarming with blatherers and always
  sure and impregnable,
The unsurvey'd interior, log-houses, clearings, wild
  animals, hunters, trappers,
Surrounding the multiform agriculture, mines, temperature,
  the gestation of new States,
Congress convening every Twelfth-month, the members
  duly coming up from the uttermost parts,
Surrounding the noble character of mechanics and farmers,
  especially the young men,
Responding their manners, speech, dress, friendships, the
  gait they have of persons who never knew how it felt
  to stand in the presence of superiors,
The freshness and candor of their physiognomy, the
  copiousness and decision of their phrenology,
The picturesque looseness of their carriage, their fierceness
  when wrong'd,
The fluency of their speech, their delight in music, their
  curiosity, good temper and open-handedness, the whole
  composite make,
The prevailing ardor and enterprise, the large amativeness,
The perfect equality of the female with the male, the
  fluid movement of the population,
The superior marine, free commerce, fisheries, whaling,
  gold-digging,
Wharf-hemm'd cities, railroad and steamboat lines
  intersecting all points,
Factories, mercantile life, labor-saving machinery, the
  Northeast, Northwest, Southwest,
Manhattan firemen, the Yankee swap, southern plantation
  life,

Slavery – the murderous, treacherous conspiracy to raise it
upon the ruins of all the rest,
On and on to the grapple with it – Assassin! then your life
or ours be the stake, and respite no more.

7

(Lo, high toward heaven, this day,
Libertad, from the conqueress' field return'd,
I mark the new aureola around your head,
No more of soft astral, but dazzling and fierce,
With war's flames and the lambent lightnings playing,
And your port immovable where you stand,
With still the inextinguishable glance and the clinch'd and
lifted fist,
And your foot on the neck of the menacing one, the
scorner utterly crush'd beneath you,
The menacing arrogant one that strode and advanced with
his senseless scorn, bearing the murderous knife,
The wide-swelling one, the braggart that would yesterday
do so much,
To-day a carrion dead and damn'd, the despised of all the
earth,
An offal rank, to the dunghill maggots spurn'd.)

8

Others take finish, but the Republic is ever constructive
and ever keeps vista,
Others adorn the past, but you O days of the present, I
adorn you,
O days of the future I believe in you – I isolate myself
for your sake,
O America because you build for mankind I build for you,

O well-beloved stone-cutters, I lead them who plan with
    decision and science,
Lead the present with friendly hand toward the future.

(Bravas to all impulses sending sane children to the next
    age!
But damn that which spends itself with no thought of the
    stain, pains, dismay, feebleness, it is bequeathing.)

9

I listened to the Phantom by Ontario's shore,
I heard the voice arising demanding bards,
By them all native and grand, by them alone can these
    States be fused into the compact organism of a Nation.

To hold men together by paper and seal or by compulsion
    is no account,
That only holds men together which aggregates all in a
    living principle, as the hold of the limbs of the body or
    the fibres of plants.

Of all races and eras these States with veins full of poetical
    stuff most need poets, and are to have the greatest, and
    use them the greatest,
Their Presidents shall not be their common referce so
    much as their poets shall.

(Soul of love and tongue of fire!
Eye to pierce the deepest deeps and sweep the world!
Ah Mother, prolific and full in all besides, yet how long
    barren, barren?)

10

Of these States the poet is the equable man,
Not in him but off from him things are grotesque,
    eccentric, fail of their full returns,
Nothing out of its place is good, nothing in its place is
    bad,
He bestows on every object or quality its fit proportion,
    neither more nor less,
He is the arbiter of the diverse, he is the key,
He is the equalizer of his age and land,
He supplies what wants supplying, he checks what wants
    checking,
In peace out of him speaks the spirit of peace, large, rich,
    thrifty, building populous towns, encouraging agriculture,
    arts, commerce, lighting the study of man, the soul,
    health, immortality, government,
In war he is the best backer of the war, he fetches artillery
    as good as the engineer's, he can make every word he
    speaks draw blood,
The years straying toward infidelity he witholds by his
    steady faith,
He is no arguer, he is judgment, (Nature accepts him
    absolutely,)
He judges not as the judge judges but as the sun falling
    round a helpless thing,
As he sees the farthest he has the most faith,
His thoughts are the hymns of the praise of things,
In the dispute on God and eternity he is silent,
He sees eternity less like a play with a prologue and
    denouement,
He sees eternity in men and women, he does not see men
    and women as dreams or dots.

For the great Idea, the idea of perfect and free individuals,
For that, the bard walks in advance, leader of leaders,
The attitude of him cheers up slaves and horrifies foreign
   despots.

Without extinction is Liberty, without retrograde is
   Equality,
They live in the feelings of young men and the best
   women,
(Not for nothing have the indomitable heads of the earth
   been always ready to fall for Liberty.)

11

For the great Idea,
That, O my brethren, that is the mission of poets.

Songs of stern defiance ever ready,
Songs of the rapid arming and the march,
The flag of peace quick-folded, and instead the flag we
   know,
Warlike flag of the great Idea.

(Angry cloth I saw there leaping!
I stand again in leaden rain your flapping folds saluting,
I sing you over all, flying beckoning through the fight – O
   the hard-contested fight!
The commons ope their rosy-flashing muzzles – the
   hurtled balls scream,
The battle-front forms amid the smoke – the volleys pour
   incessant from the line,

Hark, the ringing word *Charge!* – now the tussle and the
   furious maddening yells,
Now the corpses tumble curl'd upon the ground,

Cold, cold in death, for precious life of you,
Angry cloth I saw there leaping.)

12

Are you he who would assume a place to teach or be a poet
    here in the States?
The place is august, the terms obdurate.

Who would assume to teach here may well prepare himself
    body and mind,
He may well survey, ponder, arm, fortify, harden, make
    lithe himself,
He shall surely be question'd beforehand by me with many
    and stern questions.

Who are you indeed who would talk or sing to America?
Have you studied out the land, its idioms and men?
Have you learn'd the physiology, phrenology, politics,
    geography, pride, freedom, friendship of the land? its
    substratums and objects?
Have you consider'd the organic compact of the first day
    of the first year of Independence, sign'd by the
    Commissioners, ratified by the States, and read by
    Washington at the head of the army?
Have you possess'd yourself of the Federal Constitution?
Do you see who have left all feudal processes and poems
    behind them, and assumed the poems and processes of
    Democracy?
Are you faithful to things? do you teach what the land and
    sea, the bodies of men, womanhood, amativeness, heroic
    angers, teach?
Have you sped through fleeting customs, popularities?

Can you hold your hand against all seductions, follies,
whirls, fierce contentions? are you very strong? are you
really of the whole People?

Are you not of some coterie? some school or mere
religion?

Are you done with reviews and criticisms of life? animating
now to life itself?

Have you vivified yourself from the maternity of these
States?

Have you too the old ever-fresh forbearance and
impartiality?

Do you hold the like love for those hardening to
maturity? for the last-born? little and big? and for
the errant?

What is this you bring my America?

Is it uniform with my country?

Is it not something that has been better told or done
before?

Have you not imported this or the spirit of it in some ship?

Is it not a mere tale? a rhyme? a prettiness? – is the good
old cause in it?

Has it not dangled long at the heels of the poets,
politicians, literats, of enemies' lands?

Does it not assume that what is notoriously gone is still
here?

Does it answer universal needs? will it improve manners?

Does it sound with trumpet-voice the proud victory of the
Union in that secession war?

Can your performance face the open fields and the seaside?

Will it absorb into me as I absorb food, air, to appear
again in my strength, gait, face?

Have real employments contributed to it? original makers,
not mere amanuenses?

Does it meet modern discoveries, calibres, facts, face to
    face?
What does it mean to American persons, progresses, cities?
    Chicago, Kanada, Arkansas?
Does it see behind the apparent custodians the real
    custodians standing, menacing, silent, the mechanics,
    Manhattanese, Western men, Southerners, significant
    alike in their apathy, and in the promptness of their
    love?
Does it see what finally befalls, and has always finally
    befallen, each temporizer, patcher, outsider, partialist,
    alarmist, infidel, who has ever ask'd any thing of
    America?
What mocking and scornful negligence?
The track strew'd with the dust of skeletons,
By the roadside others disdainfully toss'd.

13

Rhymes and rhymers, pass away, poems distill'd from
    poems pass away,
The swarms of reflectors and the polite pass, and leave
    ashes,
Admirers, importers, obedient persons, make but the soil
    of literature,
America justifies itself, give it time, no disguise can deceive
    it or conceal from it, it is impassive enough,
Only toward the likes of itself will it advance to meet them,
If its poets appear it will in due time advance to meet
    them, there is no fear of mistake,
(The proof of a poet shall be sternly deferr'd till his
    country absorbs him as affectionately as he has absorb'd
    it.)

He masters whose spirit masters, he tastes sweetest who
    results sweetest in the long run,
The blood of the brawn beloved of time is unconstraint;
In the need of songs, philosophy, an appropriate native
    grand-opera, shipcraft, any craft,
He or she is greatest who contributes the greatest original
    practical example.

Already a nonchalant breed, silently emerging, appears
    on the streets,
People's lips salute only doers, lovers, satisfiers, positive
    knowers,
There will shortly be no more priests, I say their work is
    done,
Death is without emergencies here, but life is perpetual
    emergencies here,
Are your body, days, manners, superb? after death you
    shall be superb,
Justice, health, self-esteem, clear the way with irresistible
    power;
How dare you place any thing before a man?

14

Fall behind me States!
A man before all – myself, typical, before all.

Give me the pay I have served for,
Give me to sing the songs of the great Idea, take all the
    rest,
I have loved the earth, sun, animals, I have despised riches,
I have given alms to every one that ask'd, stood up for the
    stupid and crazy, devoted my income and labor to
    others,

Hated tyrants, argued not concerning God, had patience
    and indulgence toward the people, taken off my hat to
    nothing known or unknown,
Gone freely with powerful uneducated persons and with
    the young, and with the mothers of families,
Read these leaves to myself in the open air, tried them by
    trees, stars, rivers,
Dismiss'd whatever insulted my own soul or defiled my
    body,
Claim'd nothing to myself which I have not carefully
    claim'd for others on the same terms,
Sped to the camps, and comrades found and accepted from
    every State,
(Upon this breast has many a dying soldier lean'd to
    breathe his last,
This arm, this hand, this voice, have nourish'd, rais'd,
    restored,
To life recalling many a prostrate form;)
I am willing to wait to be understood by the growth of
    the taste of myself,
Rejecting none, permitting all.

(Say O Mother, have I not to your thought been faithful?
Have I not through life kept you and yours before me?)

15

I swear I begin to see the meaning of these things,
It is not the earth, it is not America who is so great,
It is I who am great or to be great, it is You up there, or
    any one,
It is to walk rapidly through civilizations, governments,
    theories,
Through poems, pageants, shows, to form individuals.

Underneath all, individuals,
I swear nothing is good to me now that ignores individuals,
The American compact is altogether with individuals,
The only government is that which makes minute of
    individuals,
The whole theory of the universe is directed unerringly to
    one single individual – namely to You.

(Mother! with subtle sense severe, with the naked sword
    in your hand,
I saw you at last refuse to treat but directly with
    individuals.)

16

Underneath all, Nativity,
I swear I will stand by my own nativity, pious or impious
    so be it;
I swear I am charm'd with nothing except nativity,
Men, women, cities, nations, are only beautiful from
    nativity.

Underneath all is the Expression of love for men and
    women,
(I swear I have seen enough of mean and impotent modes
    of expressing love for men and women,
After this day I take my own modes of expressing love for
    men and women.)

I swear I will have each quality of my race in myself,
(Talk as you like, he only suits these States whose manners
    favor the audacity and sublime turbulence of the States.)

Underneath the lessons of things, spirits, Nature,
   governments, ownerships, I swear I perceive other
   lessons,
Underneath all to me is myself, to you yourself, (the same
   monotonous old song.)

17

O I see flashing that this America is only you and me,
Its power, weapons, testimony, are you and me,
Its crimes, lies, thefts, defections, are you and me,
Its Congress is you and me, the officers, capitols, armies,
   ships, are you and me,
Its endless gestations of new States are you and me,
The war, (that war so bloody and grim, the war I will
   henceforth forget), was you and me,
Natural and artificial are you and me,
Freedom, language, poems, employments, are you and me,
Past, present, future, are you and me.

I dare not shirk any part of myself,
Not any part of America good or bad,
Not to build for that which builds for mankind,
Not to balance ranks, complexions, creeds, and the sexes,
Not to justify science nor the march of equality,
Nor to feed the arrogant blood of the brawn belov'd of
   time.

I am for those that have never been master'd,
For men and women whose tempers have never been
   master'd,
For those whom laws, theories, conventions, can never
   master.

I am for those who walk abreast with the whole earth,
Who inaugurate one to inaugurate all.

I will not be outfaced by irrational things,
I will penetrate what it is in them that is sarcastic upon
    me,
I will make cities and civilizations defer to me,
This is what I have learnt from America – it is the
    amount, and it I teach again.

(Democracy, while weapons were everywhere aim'd at
    your breast, I saw you serenely give birth to immortal
    children, saw in dreams your dilating form,
Saw you with spreading mantle covering the world.)

18

I will confront these shows of the day and night,
I will know if I am to be less than they,
I will see if I am not as majestic as they,
I will see if I am not as subtle and real as they,
I will see if I am to be less generous than they,
I will see if I have no meaning, while the houses and ships
    have meaning,
I will see if the fishes and birds are to be enough for
    themselves, and I am not to be enough for myself.

I match my spirit against yours you orbs, growths,
    mountains, brutes,
Copious as you are I absorb you all in myself, and become
    the master myself,
America isolated yet embodying all, what is it finally except
    myself?
These States, what are they except myself?

I know why the earth is gross, tantalizing, wicked, it is for
  my sake,
I take you specially to be mine, you terrible, rude forms.

(Mother, bend down, bend close to me your face,
I know not what these plots and wars and deferments are
  for,
I know not fruition's success, but I know that through war
  and crime your work goes on, and must yet go on.)

19

Thus by blue Ontario's shore,
While the winds fann'd me and the waves came trooping
  toward me,
I thrill'd with the power's pulsations, and the charm of
  my theme was upon me,
Till the tissues that held me parted their ties upon me.

And I saw the free souls of poets,
The loftiest bards of past ages strode before me,
Strange large men, long unwaked, undisclosed, were
  disclosed to me.

20

O my rapt verse, my call, mock me not!
Not for the bards of the past, not to invoke them have I
  launch'd you forth,
Not to call even those lofty bards here by Ontario's
  shores,
Have I sung so capricious and loud my savage song.

Bards for my own land only I invoke,
(For the war the war is over, the field is clear'd,)

Till they strike up marches henceforth triumphant and
    onward,
To cheer O Mother your boundless expectant soul.

Bards of the great Idea! bards of the peaceful inventions!
    (for the war, the war is over!)
Yet bards of latent armies, a million soldiers waiting
    ever-ready,
Bards with songs as from burning coals or the lightning's
    fork'd stripes!
Ample Ohio's, Kanada's bards – bards of California!
    inland bards – bards of the war!
You by my charm I invoke.

1856

This Compost

Something startles me where I thought I was safest,
I withdraw from the still woods I loved,
I will not go now on the pastures to walk,
I will not strip the clothes from my body to meet my lover
    the sea,
I will not touch my flesh to the earth as to other flesh to
    renew me.

O how can it be that the ground itself does not sicken?
How can you be alive you growths of spring?
How can you furnish health you blood of herbs, roots,
    orchards, grain?
Are they not continually putting distemper'd corpses
    within you?
Is not every continent work'd over and over with sour
    dead?

Where have you disposed of their carcasses?
Those drunkards and gluttons of so many generations?
Where have you drawn off all the foul liquid and meat?
I do not see any of it upon you to-day, or perhaps I am
    deceiv'd,
I will run a furrow with my plough, I will press my
    spade through the sod and turn it up underneath,
I am sure I shall expose some of the foul meat.

2

Behold this compost! behold it well!
Perhaps every mite has once form'd part of a sick person –
    yet behold!
The grass of spring covers the prairies,
The bean bursts noiselessly through the mould in the
    garden,
The delicate spear of the onion pierces upward,
The apple-buds cluster together on the apple-branches,
The resurrection of the wheat appears with pale visage
    out of its graves,
The tinge awakes over the willow-tree and the
    mulberry-tree,
The he-birds carol mornings and evenings while the
    she-birds sit on their nests,
The young of poultry break through the hatch'd eggs,
The new-born of animals appear, the calf is dropt from
    the cow, the colt from the mare,
Out of its little hill faithfully rise the potato's dark green
    leaves,
Out of its hill rises the yellow maize-stalk, the lilacs
    bloom in the dooryards,
The summer growth is innocent and disdainful above all
    those strata of sour dead.

What chemistry!
That the winds are really not infectious,
That this is no cheat, this transparent green-wash of the
    sea which is so amorous after me,
That it is safe to allow it to lick my naked body all over
    with its tongues,
That i t will not endanger me with the fevers that have
    deposited themselves in it,

That all is clean forever and forever,
That the cool drink from the well tastes so good,
That blackberries are so flavorous and juicy,
That the fruits of the apple-orchard and the orange-orchard,
    that melons, grapes, peaches, plums, will none of them
    poison me,
That when I recline on the grass I do not catch any disease,
Though probably every spear of grass rises out of what was
    once a catching disease.

Now I am terrified at the Earth, it is that calm and patient,
It grows such sweet things out of such corruptions,
It turns harmless and stainless on its axis, with such endless
    successions of diseas'd corpses,
It distils such exquisite winds out of such infused fetor,
It renews with such unwitting looks its prodigal, annual,
    sumptuous crops,
It gives such divine materials to men, and accepts such
    leavings from them at last.

1856

Kosmos

Who includes diversity and is Nature,

Who is the amplitude of the earth, and the coarseness and
sexuality of the earth, and the great charity of the earth,
and the equilibrium also,

Who has not look'd forth from the windows the eyes for
nothing, or whose brain held audience with messengers
for nothing,

Who contains believers and disbelievers, who is the most
majestic lover,

Who holds duly his or her triune proportion of realism,
spiritualism, and of the æsthetic or intellectual,

Who having consider'd the body finds all its organs and
parts good,

Who, out of the theory of the earth and of his or her body
understands by subtle analogies all other theories,

The theory of a city, a poem, and of the large politics of
these States;

Who believes not only in our globe with its sun and moon,
but in other globes with their suns and moons,

Who, constructing the house of himself or herself, not for
a day but for all time, sees races, eras, dates, generations,

The past, the future, dwelling there, like space, inseparable
together.

1860

The Sleepers

I

I wander all night in my vision,
Stepping with light feet . . . swiftly and noiselessly stepping
   and stopping,
Bending with open eyes over the shut eyes of sleepers;
Wandering and confused . . . lost to myself . . .
   ill-assorted . . . contradictory,
Pausing and gazing and bending and stopping.

How solemn they look there, stretched and still;
How quiet they breathe, the little children in their cradles.

The wretched features of ennuyees, the white features of
   corpses, the livid faces of drunkards, the sick-gray
   faces of onanists,
The gashed bodies on battlefields, the insane in their
   strong-doored rooms, the sacred idiots,
The newborn emerging from gates and the dying emerging
   from gates,
The night pervades them and enfolds them.

The married couple sleep calmly in their bed, he with his
   palm on the hip of the wife, and she with her palm
   on the hip of the husband,
The sisters sleep lovingly side by side in their bed,
The men sleep lovingly side by side in theirs,
And the mother sleeps with her little child carefully
   wrapped.

The blind sleep, and the deaf and dumb sleep,
The prisoner sleeps well in the prison . . . the runaway
   son sleeps,

The murderer that is to be hung next day ... how does he
    sleep?
And the murdered person ... how does he sleep?

The female that loves unrequited sleeps,
And the male that loves unrequited sleeps;
The head of the moneymaker that plotted all day sleeps,
And the enraged and treacherous dispositions sleep.

I stand with drooping eyes by the worstsuffering and
    restless,
I pass my hands soothingly to and fro a few inches from
    them;
The restless sink in their beds ... they fitfully sleep.

The earth recedes from me into the night,
I saw that it was beautiful ... and I see that what is not
    the earth is beautiful.

I go from bedside to bedside ... I sleep close with the
    other sleepers, each in turn;
I dream in my dream all the dreams of the other dreamers,
And I become the other dreamers.

I am a dance ... Play up there! the fit is whirling me fast.

I am the everlaughing ... it is new moon and twilight,
I see the hiding of douceurs ... I see nimble ghosts
    whichever way I look,
Cache and cache again deep in the ground and sea, and
    where it is neither ground or sea.

Well do they do their jobs, those journeymen divine,
Only from me can they hide nothing and would not if
    they could;

I reckon I am their boss, and they make me a pet besides,
And surround me, and lead me and run ahead when I walk,
And lift their cunning covers and signify me with stretched
    arms, and resume the way;
Onward we move, a gay gang of blackguards with
    mirthshouting music and wildflapping pennants of joy.

I am the actor and the actress . . . the voter . . . the
    politician,
The emigrant and the exile . . . the criminal that stood in
    the box,
He who has been famous, and he who shall be famous after
    today,
The stammerer . . . the wellformed person . . . the wasted
    or feeble person.

I am she who adorned herself and folded her hair
    expectantly,
My truant lover has come and it is dark.

Double yourself and receive me darkness,
Receive me and my lover too . . . he will not let me go
    without him.

I roll myself upon you as upon a bed . . . I resign myself
    to the dusk.

He whom I call answers me and takes the place of my
    lover,
He rises with me silently from the bed.

Darkness you are gentler than my lover . . . his flesh was
    sweaty and panting,
I feel the hot moisture yet that he left me.

My hands are spread forth ... I pass them in all
    directions,
I would sound up the shadowy shore to which you are
    journeying.

Be careful, darkness ... already, what was it touched me?
I thought my lover had gone ... else darkness and he are
    one,
I hear the heart-beat ... I follow ... I fade away.

O hotcheeked and blushing! O foolish hectic!
O for pity's sake, no one must see me now! ... my clothes
    were stolen while I was abed,
Now I am thrust forth, where shall I run?

Pier that I saw dimly last night when I looked from the
    windows,
Pier out from the main, let me catch myself with you and
    stay ... I will not chafe you;
I feel ashamed to go naked about the world,
And am curious to know where my feet stand ... and what
    is this flooding me, childhood or manhood ... and the
    hunger that crosses the bridge between.

The cloth laps a first sweet eating and drinking,
Laps life-swelling yolks ... laps ear of rose-corn, milky
    and just ripened:
The white teeth stay, and the boss-tooth advances in
    darkness,
And liquor is spilled on lips and bosoms by touching
    glasses, and the best liquor afterward.

2

I descend my western course ... my sinews are flaccid,
Perfume and youth course through me, and I am their
    wake.

It is my face yellow and wrinkled instead of the old
    woman's,
I sit low in a strawbottom chair and carefully darn my
    grandson's stockings.

It is I too ... the sleepless widow looking out on the
    winter midnight,
I see the sparkles of starshine on the icy and pallid earth.

A shroud I see – and I am the shroud ... I wrap a body
    and lie in the coffin;
It is dark here underground ... it is not evil or pain here
    ... it is blank here, for reasons.

It seems to me that everything in the light and air ought
    to be happy;
Whoever is not in his coffin and the dark grave, let him
    know he has enough.

3

I see a beautiful gigantic swimmer swimming naked
    through the eddies of the sea,
His brown hair lies close and even to his head ... he
    strikes out with courageous arms ... he urges himself
    with his legs.

I see his white body ... I see his undaunted eyes;
I hate the swift-running eddies that would dash him
   headforemost on the rocks.

What are you doing you ruffianly red-trickled waves?
Will you kill the courageous giant? Will you kill him in the
   prime of his middle age?

Steady and long he struggles;
He is baffled and banged and bruised ... he holds out
   while his strength holds out,
The slapping eddies are spotted with his blood ... they
   bear him away ... they roll him and swing him and
   turn him:
His beautiful body is borne in the circling eddies ... it is
   continually bruised on rocks,
Swiftly and out of sight is borne the brave corpse.

4

I turn but do not extricate myself;
Confused ... a pastreading ... another, but with
   darkness yet.

The beach is cut by the razory ice-wind ... the wreck-guns
   sound,
The tempest lulls and the moon comes floundering through
   the drifts.

I look where the ship helplessly heads end on ... I hear
   the burst as she strikes ... I hear the howls of dismay
   ... they grow fainter and fainter.

I cannot aid with my wringing fingers;
I can but rush to the surf and let it drench me and freeze
   upon me.

I search with the crowd . . . not one of the company is
   washed to us alive;
In the morning I help pick up the dead and lay them in
   rows in a barn.

5

Now of the old war-days . . . the defeat at Brooklyn;
Washington stands inside the lines . . . he stands on the
   entrenched hills amid a crowd of officers,
His face is cold and damp . . . he cannot repress the
   weeping drops . . . he lifts the glass perpetually to his
   eyes . . . the color is blanched from his cheeks,
He sees the slaughter of the southern braves confided to
   him by their parents.

The same at last and at last when peace is declared,
He stands in the room of the old tavern . . . the
   wellbeloved soldiers all pass through.

The officers speechless and slow draw near in their turns,
The chief encircles their necks with his arm and kisses
   them on the cheek,
He kisses lightly the wet cheeks one after another . . . he
   shakes hands and bids goodbye to the army.

6

Now I tell what my mother told me today as we sat at
   dinner together,
Of when she was a nearly grown girl living home with
   her parents on the old homestead.

A red squaw came one breakfastime to the old homestead,
On her back she carried a bundle of rushes for
rushbottoming chairs;
Her hair straight shiny coarse black and profuse
halfenveloped her face,
Her step was free and elastic . . . her voice sounded
exquisitely as she spoke.

My mother looked in delight and amazement at the
stranger,
She looked at the beauty of her tallborne face and full and
pliant limbs,
The more she looked upon her she loved her,
Never before had she seen such wonderful beauty and
purity;
She made her sit on a bench by the jamb of the fireplace
. . . she cooked food for her,
She had no work to give her but she gave her
remembrance and fondness.

The red squaw staid all the forenoon, and toward the
middle of the afternoon she went away;
O my mother was loth to have her go away,
All the week she thought of her . . . she watched for her
many a month,
She remembered her many a winter and many a summer,
But the red squaw never came nor was heard of there
again.

Now Lucifer was not dead . . . or if he was I am his
sorrowful terrible heir;
I have been wronged . . . I am oppressed . . . I hate him
that oppresses me,
I will either destroy him, or he shall release me.

Damn him! how he does defile me,

How he informs against my brother and sister and takes
    pay for their blood,

How he laughs when I look down the bend after the
    steamboat that carries away my woman.

Now the vast dusk bulk that is the whale's bulk . . . it
    seems mine,

Warily, sportsman! though I lie so sleepy and sluggish,
    my tap is death.

7

A show of the summer softness . . . a contact of something
    unseen . . . an amour of the light and air;

I am jealous and overwhelmed with friendliness,

And will go gallivant with the light and the air myself,

And have an unseen something to be in contact with them
    also.

O love and summer! you are in the dreams and in me,

Autumn and winter are in the dreams . . . the farmer goes
    with his thrift,

The droves and crops increase . . . the barns are wellfilled.

Elements merge in the night . . . ships make tacks in the
    dreams . . . the sailor sails . . . the exile returns home,

The fugitive returns unharmed . . . the immigrant is back
    beyond months and years;

The poor Irishman lives in the simple house of his
    childhood, with the wellknown neighbors and faces,

They warmly welcome him . . . he is barefoot again . . . he
    forgets he is welloff;

The Dutchman voyages home, and the Scotchman and
    Welchman voyage home . . . and the native of the
    Mediterranean voyages home;

To every port of England and France and Spain enter
    wellfilled ships;
The Swiss foots it toward his hills . . . the Prussian goes
    his way, and the Hungarian his way, and the Pole goes
    his way,
The Swede returns, and the Dane and Norwegian return.

The homeward bound and the outward bound,
The beautiful lost swimmer, the ennuyé, the onanist,
    the female that loves unrequited, the moneymaker,
The actor and actress . . . those through with their parts
    and those waiting to commence,
The affectionate boy, the husband and wife, the voter, the
    nominee that is chosen and the nominee that has failed,
The great already known, and the great anytime after to
    day,
The stammerer, the sick, the perfectformed, the homely,
The criminal that stood in the box, the judge that sat and
    sentenced him, the fluent lawyers, the jury, the audience,
The laugher and weeper, the dancer, the midnight widow,
    the red squaw,
The consumptive, the erysipalite, the idiot, he that is
    wronged,
The antipodes, and every one between this and them in the
    dark,
I swear they are averaged now . . . one is no better than
    the other,
The night and sleep have likened them and restored them.

I swear they are all beautiful,
Every one that sleeps is beautiful . . . every thing in the
    dim night is beautiful,
The wildest and bloodiest is over and all is peace.

Peace is always beautiful,
The myth of heaven indicates peace and night.

The myth of heaven indicates the soul;
The soul is always beautiful . . . it appears more or it
  appears less . . . it comes or lags behind,
It comes from its embowered garden and looks pleasantly
  on itself and encloses the world;
Perfect and clean the genitals previously jetting, and
  perfect and clean the womb cohering,
The head wellgrown and proportioned and plumb, and
  the bowels and joints proportioned and plumb.

The soul is always beautiful,
The universe is duly in order . . . every thing is in its
  place,
What is arrived is in its place, and what waits is in its
  place;
The twisted skull waits . . . the watery or rotten blood
  waits,
The child of the glutton or venerealee waits long, and the
  child of the drunkard waits long, and the drunkard
  himself waits long,
The sleepers that lived and died wait . . . the far advanced
  are to go on in their turns, and the far behind are to go
  on in their turns,
The diverse shall be no less diverse, but they shall flow
  and unite . . . they unite now.

8

The sleepers are very beautiful as they lie unclothed,
They flow hand in hand over the whole earth from east to
  west as they lie unclothed;

The Asiatic and African are hand in hand . . . the
  European and American are hand in hand,
Learned and unlearned are hand in hand . . . and male and
  female are hand in hand;
The bare arm of the girl crosses the bare breast of her
  lover . . . they press close without lust . . . his lips press
  her neck,
The father holds his grown or ungrown son in his arms
  with measureless love . . . and the son holds the father
  in his arms with measureless love,
The white hair of the mother shines on the white wrist of
  the daughter,
The breath of the boy goes with the breath of the man
  . . . friend is inarmed by friend,
The scholar kisses the teacher and the teacher kisses the
  scholar . . . the wronged is made right,
The call of the slave is one with the master's call . . .
  and the master salutes the slave,
The felon steps forth from the prison . . . the insane
  becomes sane . . . the suffering of sick persons is
  relieved,
The sweatings and fevers stop . . . the throat that was
  unsound is sound . . . the lungs of the consumptive are
  resumed . . . the poor distressed head is free,
The joints of the rheumatic move as smoothly as ever, and
  smoother than ever,
Stiflings and passages open . . . the paralysed become
  supple,
The swelled and convulsed and congested awake to
  themselves in condition,
They pass the invigoration of the night and the chemistry
  of the night and awake.

I too pass from the night;

I stay awhile away O night, but I return to you again and
  love you;

Why should I be afraid to trust myself to you?

I am not afraid . . . I have been well brought forward
  by you;

I love the rich running day, but I do not desert her in
  whom I lay so long:

I know not how I came of you, and I know not where I
  go with you . . . but I know I came well and shall go
  well.

I will stop only a time with the night . . . and rise betimes.

I will duly pass the day O my mother and duly return to
  you;

Not you will yield forth the dawn again more surely than
  you will yield forth me again,

Not the womb yields the babe in its time more surely than
  I shall be yielded from you in my time.

1855

To Think of Time

1

To think of time – of all that retrospection,
To think of to-day, and the ages continued henceforward.

Have you guess'd you yourself would not continue?
Have you dreaded these earth-beetles?
Have you fear'd the future would be nothing to you?

Is to-day nothing? is the beginningless past nothing?
If the future is nothing they are just as surely nothing.

To think that the sun rose in the east – that men and
    women were flexible, real, alive – that every thing was
    alive,
To think that you and I did not see, feel, think, nor bear
    our part,
To think that we are now here and bear our part.

2

Not a day passes, not a minute or second without an
    accouchement,
Not a day passes, not a minute or second without a corpse.

The dull nights go over and the dull days also,
The soreness of lying so much in bed goes over,
The physician after long putting off gives the silent and
    terrible look for an answer,
The children come hurried and weeping, and the brothers
    and sisters are sent for,

Medicines stand unused on the shelf, (the camphor-smell
   has long pervaded the rooms,)
The faithful hand of the living does not desert the hand of
   the dying,
The twitching lips press lightly on the forehead of the
   dying,
The breath ceases and the pulse of the heart ceases,
The corpse stretches on the bed and the living look upon
   it,
It is palpable as the living are palpable.

The living look upon the corpse with their eyesight,
But without eyesight lingers a different living and looks
   curiously on the corpse.

3

To think the thought of death merged in the thought of
   materials,
To think of all these wonders of city and country, and
   others taking great interest in them, and we taking no
   interest in them.

To think how eager we are in building our houses,
To think others shall be just as eager, and we quite
   indifferent.

(I see one building the house that serves him a few years,
   or seventy or eighty years at most,
I see one building the house that serves him longer than
   that.)

Slow-moving and black lines creep over the whole earth –
   they never cease – they are the burial lines,
He that was President was buried, and he that is now
   President shall surely be buried.

4

A reminiscence of the vulgar fate,
A frequent sample of the life and death of workmen,
Each after his kind.

Cold dash of waves at the ferry-wharf, posh and ice in the
    river, half-frozen mud in the streets,
A gray discouraged sky overhead, the short last daylight
    of December,
A hearse and stages, the funeral of an old Broadway
    stage-driver, the cortege mostly drivers.

Steady the trot to the cemetery, duly rattles the death-bell,
The gate is pass'd, the new-dug grave is halted at, the
    living alight, the hearse uncloses,
The coffin is pass'd out, lower'd and settled, the whip is
    laid on the coffin, the earth is swiftly shovel'd in,
The mound above is flatted with the spades – silence,
A minute – no one moves or speaks – it is done,
He is decently put away – is there any thing more?

He was a good fellow, free-mouth'd, quick temper'd,
    not bad-looking,
Ready with life or death for a friend, fond of women,
    gambled, ate hearty, drank hearty,
Had known what it was to be flush, grew low-spirited
    toward the last, sicken'd, was help'd by a contribution,
Died, aged forty-one years – and that was his funeral.

Thumb extended, finger uplifted, apron, cape, gloves,
    strap, wet-weather clothes, whip carefully chosen,
Boss, spotter, starter, hostler, somebody loafing on you,
    you loafing on somebody, headway, man before and man
    behind,

Good day's work, bad day's work, pet stock, mean stock,
  first out, last out, turning-in at night,
To think that these are so much and so nigh to other
  drivers, and he there takes no interest in them.

5

The markets, the government, the working-man's wages,
  to think what account they are through our nights and
  days,
To think that other working-men will make just as great
  account of them, yet we make little or no account.

The vulgar and the refined, what you call sin and what
  you call goodness, to think how wide a difference,
To think the difference will still continue to others, yet we
  lie beyond the difference.

To think how much pleasure there is,
Do you enjoy yourself in the city? or engaged in business?
  or planning a nomination and election? or with your
  wife and family?
Or with your mother and sisters? or in womanly
  housework? or the beautiful maternal cares?
These also flow onward to others, you and I flow onward,
But in due time you and I shall take less interest in them.

Your farm, profits, crops – to think how engross'd you are,
To think there will still be farms, profits, crops, yet for
  you of what avail?

6

What will be will be well, for what is is well,
To take interest is well, and not to take interest shall be
  well.

The domestic joys, the daily housework or business, the
   building of houses, are not phantasms, they have
   weight, form, location,
Farms, profits, crops, markets, wages, government, are
   none of them phantasms,
The difference between sin and goodness is no delusion,
The earth is not an echo, man and his life and all the
   things of his life are well-consider'd.

You are not thrown to the winds, you gather certainly
   and safely around yourself,
Yourself! yourself! yourself, for ever and ever!

7

It is not to diffuse you that you were born of your mother
   and father, it is to identify you,
It is not that you should be undecided, but that you should
   be decided,
Something long preparing and formless is arrived and
   form'd in you,
You are henceforth secure, whatever comes or goes.

The threads that were spun are gather'd, the weft crosses
   the warp, the pattern is systematic.

The preparations have every one been justified,
The orchestra have sufficiently tuned their instruments,
   the baton has given the signal.

The guest that was coming, he waited long, he is now
   housed,
He is one of those who are beautiful and happy, he is one
   of those that to look upon and be with is enough.

The law of the past cannot be eluded,
The law of the present and future cannot be eluded,
The law of the living cannot be eluded, it is eternal,
The law of promotion and transformation cannot be eluded,
The law of heroes and good-doers cannot be eluded,
The law of drunkards, informers, mean persons, not one
    iota thereof can be eluded.

8

Slow moving and black lines go ceaselessly over the earth,
Northerner goes carried and Southerner goes carried, and
    they on the Atlantic side and they on the Pacific,
And they between, and all through the Mississippi
    country, and all over the earth.

The great masters and kosmos are well as they go, the
    heroes and good-doers are well,
The known leaders and inventors and the rich owners and
    pious and distinguish'd may be well,
But there is more account than that, there is strict account
    of all.

The interminable hordes of the ignorant and wicked are
    not nothing,
The barbarians of Africa and Asia are not nothing,
The perpetual successions of shallow people are not nothing
    as they go.

Of and in all these things,
I have dream'd that we are not to be changed so much, nor
    the law of us changed,
I have dream'd that heroes and good-doers shall be under
    the present and past law,

And that murderers, drunkards, liars, shall be under the
    present and past law,
For I have dream'd that the law they are under now is
    enough.

And I have dream'd that the purpose and essence of the
    known life, the transient,
Is to form and decide identity for the unknown life, the
    permanent.

If all came but to ashes of dung,
If maggots and rats ended us, then Alarum! for we are
    betray'd,
Then indeed suspicion of death.

Do you suspect death? if I were to suspect death I should
    die now,
Do you think I could walk pleasantly and well-suited
    toward annihilation?

Pleasantly and well-suited I walk,
Whither I walk I cannot define, but I know it is good,
The whole universe indicates that it is good,
The past and the present indicate that it is good.

How beautiful and perfect are the animals!
How perfect the earth, and the minutest thing upon it!
What is called good is perfect, and what is called bad is
    just as perfect,
The vegetables and minerals are all perfect, and the
    imponderable fluids perfect;
Slowly and surely they have pass'd on to this, and slowly
    and surely they yet pass on.

9

I swear I think now that every thing without exception
    has an eternal soul!
The trees have, rooted in the ground! the weeds of the sea
    have! the animals!

I swear I think there is nothing but immortality!
That the exquisite scheme is for it, and the nebulous float
    is for it, and the cohering is for it!
And all preparation is for it – and identity is for it – and
    life and materials are altogether for it!

1855

A Noiseless Patient Spider

A noiseless patient spider,
I mark'd where on a little promontory it stood isolated,
Mark'd how to explore the vacant vast surrounding,
It launch'd forth filament, filament, filament, out of itself,
Ever unreeling them, ever tirelessly speeding them.

And you O my soul where you stand,
Surrounded, detached, in measureless oceans of space,
Ceaselessly musing, venturing, throwing, seeking the
    spheres to connect them,
Till the bridge you wil need be form'd, till the ductile
    anchor hold,
Till the gossamer thread you fling catch somewhere, O my
    soul.

1868

You Tides with Ceaseless Swell

You tides with ceaseless swell! you power that does this
    work!
You unseen force, centripetal, centrifugal, through space's
    spread,
Rapport of sun, moon, earth, and all the constellations,
What are the messages by you from distant stars to us?
    what Sirius'? what Capella's?
What central heart – and you the pulse – vivifies all? what
    boundless aggregate of all?
What subtle indirection and significance in you? what clue
    to all in you? what fluid, vast identity,
Holding the universe with all its parts as one – as sailing
    in a ship?

1885

Good-bye My Fancy!

Good-bye my Fancy!
Farewell dear mate, dear love!
I'm going away, I know not where,
Or to what fortune, or whether I may ever see you again,
So Good-bye my Fancy.

Now for my last – let me look back a moment;
The slower fainter ticking of the clock is in me,
Exit, nightfall, and soon the heart-thud stopping.

Long have we lived, joy'd, caress'd together;
Delightful! – now separation – Good-bye my Fancy.

You let me not be too hasty,
Long indeed have we lived, slept, filter'd, become really
   blended into one;
Then if we die we die together, (yes, we'll remain one,)
If we go anywhere we'll go together to meet what happens,
May-be we'll be better off and blither, and learn something,
May-be it is yourself now really ushering me to the true
   songs, (who knows?)
May-be it is you the mortal knob really undoing,
   turning – so now finally,
Good-bye – and hail! my Fancy.

1891

Respondez!*

RESPONDEZ! Respondez!
(The war is completed – the price is paid – the title is
   settled beyond recall;)
Let every one answer! let those who sleep be waked! let
   none evade!
Must we still go on with our affectations and sneaking?
Let me bring this to a close – I pronounce openly for a
   new distribution of roles;
Let that which stood in front go behind! and let that which
   was behind advance to the front and speak;
Let murderers, bigots, fools, unclean persons, offer new
   propositions!
Let the old propositions be postponed!
Let faces and theories be turn'd inside out! let meanings
   be freely criminal, as well as results!
Let there be no suggestion above the suggestion of
   drudgery!
Let none be pointed toward his destination! (Say! do you
   know your destination?)
Let men and women be mock'd with bodies and mock'd
   with Souls!
Let the love that waits in them, wait! let it die, or pass
   still-born to other spheres!
Let the sympathy that waits in every man, wait! or let it
   also pass, a dwarf, to other spheres!
Let contradictions prevail! let one thing contradict
   another! and let one line of my poems contradict
   another!
Let the people sprawl with yearning, aimless hands! let

*Note: This poem was excluded by Whitman from the final
edition.

their tongues be broken! let their eyes be discouraged!
  let none descend into their hearts with the fresh
  lusciousness of love!
(Stifled, O days! O lands! in every public and private
  corruption!
Smother'd in thievery, impotence, shamelessness,
  mountain-high;
Brazen effrontery, scheming, rolling like ocean's waves
  around and upon you, O my days! my lands!
For not even those thunderstorms, nor fiercest lightnings
  of the war, have purified the atmosphere;)
– Let the theory of America still be management, caste,
  comparison! (Say! what other theory would you?)
Let them that distrust birth and death still lead the rest!
  (Say! why shall they not lead you?)
Let the crust of hell be neared and trod on! let the days
  be darker than the nights! let slumber bring less slumber
  than waking time brings!
Let the world never appear to him or her for whom it was
  all made!
Let the heart of the young man still exile itself from the
  heart of the old man! and let the heart of the old man be
  exiled from that of the young man!
Let the sun and moon go! let scenery take the applause of
  the audience! let there be apathy under the stars!
Let freedom prove no man's inalienable right! every one
  who can tyrannize, let him tyrannize to his satisfaction!
Let none but infidels be countenanced!
Let the eminence of meanness, treachery, sarcasm, hate,
  greed, indecency, impotence, lust, be taken for granted
  above all! let writers, judges, governments, households,
  religions, philosophies, take such for granted above all!
Let the worst men beget children out of the worst women!
Let the priest still play at immortality!

Let death be inaugurated!

Let nothing remain but the ashes of teachers, artists,
    moralists, lawyers, and learn'd and polite persons!

Let him who is without my poems be assassinated!

Let the cow, the horse, the camel, the garden-bee – let the
    mud-fish, the lobster, the mussel, eel, the sting-ray, and
    the grunting pig-fish – let these, and the like of these,
    be put on a perfect equality with man and woman!

Let churches accommodate serpents, vermin, and the
    corpses of those who have died of the most filthy of
    diseases!

Let marriage slip down among fools, and be for none but
    fools!

Let men among themselves talk and think forever obscenely
    of women! and let women among themselves talk and
    think obscenely of men!

Let us all, without missing one, be exposed in public,
    naked, monthly, at the peril of our lives! let our bodies
    be freely handled and examined by whoever chooses!

Let nothing but copies at second hand be permitted to
    exist upon the earth!

Let the earth desert God, nor let there ever henceforth
    be mention'd the name of God!

Let there be no God!

Let there be money, business, imports, exports, custom,
    authority, precedents, pallor, dyspepsia, smut, ignorance,
    unbelief!

Let judges and criminals be transposed! let the
    prison-keepers be put in prison! let those that were
    prisoners take the keys! (Say! why might they not just
    as well be transposed?)

Let the slaves be masters! let the masters become slaves!

Let the reformers descend from the stands where they are

forever bawling! let an idiot or insane person appear on
each of the stands!

Let the Asiatic, the African, the European, the American,
and the Australian, go armed against the murderous
stealthiness of each other! let them sleep armed! let none
believe in good will!

Let there be no unfashionable wisdom! let such be scorn'd
and derided off from the earth!

Let a floating cloud in the sky – let a wave of the sea – let
growing mint, spinach, onions, tomatoes – let these be
exhibited as shows, at a great price for admission!

Let all the men of These States stand aside for a few
smouchers! let the few seize on what they choose! let
the rest gawk, giggle, starve, obey!

Let shadows be furnish'd with genitals! let substances be
deprived of their genitals!

Let there be wealthy and immense cities – but still through
any of them, not a single poet, savior, knower, lover!

Let the infidels of These States laugh all faith away!

If one man be found who has faith, let the rest set upon
him!

Let them affright faith! let them destroy the power of
breeding faith!

Let the she-harlots and the he-harlots be prudent! let them
dance on, while seeming lasts! (O seeming! seeming!
seeming!)

Let the preachers recite creeds! let them still teach only
what they have been taught!

Let insanity still have charge of sanity!

Let books take the place of trees, animals, rivers, clouds!

Let the daub'd portraits of heroes supersede heroes!

Let the manhood of man never take steps after itself!

Let it take steps after eunuchs, and after consumptive
and genteel persons!

Let the white person again tread the black person under
   his heel! (Say which is trodden under heel, after all?)
Let the reflections of the things of the world be studied
   in mirrors! let the things themselves still continue
   unstudied!
Let a man seek pleasure everywhere except in himself!
Let a woman seek happiness everywhere except in herself!
(What real happiness have you had one single hour through
   your whole life?)
Let the limited years of life do nothing for the limitless
   years of death! (What do you suppose death will do,
   then?)

1856

Debris*

*

He is wisest who has the most caution,
He only wins who goes far enough.

*

Any thing is as good as established, when that is established
   that will produce it and continue it.

*

What General has a good army in himself, has a good army;
He happy in himself, or she happy in herself, is happy,
But I tell you you cannot be happy by others, any more
   than you can beget or conceive a child by others.

*

Have you learned lessons only of those who admired you,
   and were tender with you, and stood aside for you?
Have you not learned the great lessons of those who rejected
   you, and braced themselves against you? or who treated
   you with contempt, or disputed the passage with you?
Have you had no practice to receive opponents when they
   come?

*

Despairing cries float ceaselessly toward me, day and night,
The sad voice of Death – the call of my nearest lover,
   putting forth, alarmed, uncertain,
This sea I am quickly to sail, come tell me,
Come tell me where I am speeding – tell me my destination.

   Note: This poem was excluded by Whitman from the final edition.

*

I understand your anguish, but I cannot help you,
I approach, hear, behold – the sad mouth, the look out
    of the eyes, your mute inquiry,
Whither I go from the bed I now recline on, come tell me ;
Old age, alarmed, uncertain – A young woman's voice
    appealing to me, for comfort,
A young man's voice, *Shall I not escape ?*

*

A thousand perfect men and women appear,
Around each gathers a cluster of friends, and gay children
    and youths, with offerings.

*

A mask – a perpetual natural disguiser of herself,
Concealing her face, concealing her form,
Changes and transformations every hour, every moment,
Falling upon her even when she sleeps.

*

One sweeps by, attended by an immense train,
All emblematic of peace – not a soldier or menial among
    them.

*

One sweeps by, old, with black eyes, and profuse white
    hair,
He has the simple magnificence of health and strength,
His face strikes as with flashes of lightning whoever it
    turns toward.

*

Three old men slowly pass, followed by three others, and
  they by three others,
They are beautiful – The one in the middle of each group
  holds his companions by the hand,
As they walk, they give out perfume wherever they walk.

*

Women sit, or move to and fro – some old, some young,
The young are beautiful – but the old are more beautiful
  than the young.

*

What weeping face is that looking from the window?
Why does it stream those sorrowful tears?
Is it for some burial place, vast and dry?
Is it to wet the soil of graves?

*

I will take an egg out of the robin's nest in the orchard,
I will take a branch of gooseberries from the old bush in
  the garden, and go and preach to the world;
You shall see I will not meet a single heretic or scorner,
You shall see how I stump clergymen, and confound them,
You shall see me showing a scarlet tomato, and a white
  pebble from the beach.

*

Behavior – fresh, native, copious, each one for himself or
  herself,
Nature and the Soul expressed – America and freedom
  expressed – In it the finest art,
In it pride, cleanliness, sympathy, to have their chance,

In it physique, intellect, faith – in it just as much as to
  manage an army or a city, or to write a book – perhaps
  more,
The youth, the laboring person, the poor person, rivalling
  all the rest – perhaps outdoing the rest,
The effects of the universe no greater than its;
For there is nothing in the whole universe that can be
  more effective than a man's or woman's daily behavior
  can be,
In any position, in any one of These States.

*

Not the pilot has charged himself to bring his ship into
  port, though beaten back, and many times baffled,
Not the path-finder, penetrating inland, weary and long,
By deserts parched, snows chilled, rivers wet, perseveres
  till he reaches his destination,
More than I have charged myself, heeded or unheeded, to
  compose a free march for These States,
To be exhilarating music to them, years, centuries hence.

*

I thought I was not alone, walking here by the shore,
But the one I thought was with me, as now I walk by the
  shore,
As I lean and look through the glimmering light – that
  one has utterly disappeared,
And those appear that perplex me.

1860

More about Penguins

Penguinews, which appears every month, contains details of all the new books issued by Penguins as they are published. From time to time it is supplemented by *Penguins in Print*, which is a complete list of all available books published by Penguins. (There are well over three thousand of these.)

A specimen copy of *Penguinews* will be sent to you free on request, and you can become a subscriber for the price of the postage. For a year's issues (including the complete lists) please send 30p if you live in the United Kingdom, or 60p if you live elsewhere. Just write to Dept EP, Penguin Books Ltd, Harmondsworth, Middlesex, enclosing a cheque or postal order and your name will be added to the mailing list.

Note: *Penguinews* and *Penguins in Print* are not available in the U.S.A. or Canada

POET TO POET

In the introductions to their personal selections from the work of poets they have admired, the individual editors write as follows:

Crabbe Selected by C. Day Lewis

'As his poetry displays a balance and decorum in its versification, so his moral ideal is a kind of normality to which every civilized being should aspire. This, when one looks at the desperate expedients and experiments of poets (and others) today, is at least refreshing.'

Wordsworth Selected by Lawrence Durrell

'Wordsworth almost more than any other English poet enjoyed a sense of inner confirmation – the mysterious sense of election to poetry as a whole way of life. He realized too that one cannot condescend to nature – one must work for it like a monk over a missal which he will not live to see finished.'

Tennyson Selected by Kingsley Amis

'England notoriously had its doubts as well as its certainties, its neuroses as well as its moral health, its fits of gloom and frustration and panic as well as its complacency. Tennyson is the voice of those doubts and their accompaniments, and his genius enabled him to communicate them in such a way that we can understand them and feel them as our own. In short we know from experience just what he means. Eliot called him the saddest of all English poets, and I cannot improve on that judgement.'

Also available

Henryson *Selected by Hugh MacDiarmid*
Herbert *Selected by W. H. Auden*